Using Talk to
Support Writing

Education at SAGE

SAGE is a leading international publisher of journals, books, and electronic media for academic, educational, and professional markets.

Our education publishing includes:

- accessible and comprehensive texts for aspiring education professionals and practitioners looking to further their careers through continuing professional development

- inspirational advice and guidance for the classroom

- authoritative state of the art reference from the leading authors in the field

Find out more at: **www.sagepub.co.uk/education**

Using Talk to Support Writing

Ros Fisher, Susan Jones, Shirley Larkin and
Debra Myhill

SAGE

Los Angeles | London | New Delhi
Singapore | Washington DC

SAGE Publications Ltd
1 Oliver's Yard
55 City Road
London EC1Y 1SP

SAGE Publications Inc.
2455 Teller Road
Thousand Oaks, California 91320

SAGE Publications India Pvt Ltd
B 1/I 1 Mohan Cooperative Industrial Area
Mathura Road
New Delhi 110 044

SAGE Publications Asia-Pacific Pte Ltd
33 Pekin Street #02-01
Far East Square
Singapore 048763

Library of Congress Control Number: 2009937360

British Library Cataloguing in Publication data

A catalogue record for this book is available from the British Library

ISBN 978-1-84920-143-8
ISBN 978-1-84920-144-5 (pbk)

Typeset by C&M Digitals, Pvt Ltd, Chennai, India
Printed in Great Britain by MPG Group, Bodmin, Cornwall
Printed on paper from sustainable resources

Mixed Sources
Product group from well-managed
forests and other controlled sources
www.fsc.org Cert no. SA-COC-1565
© 1996 Forest Stewardship Council
FSC

Contents

About the authors   vii
Introduction   **viii**
Classroom poster   **xii**

1   Learning to write   **1**
Debra Myhill

2   Exploring classroom talk through action research   **20**
Susan Jones

Interlude 1   Being involved in research – the view from
a school   Frances Dunkin   34

3   Talk to generate ideas   **38**
Ros Fisher

Lesson plans for idea generation   56
    Conscience alley   56
    Forum theatre   58
    Freeze-frame   60
    Using music   62

4   Writing aloud – the role of oral rehearsal   **64**
Debra Myhill

Interlude 2   Using write aloud in the classroom   Rachael Milsom   80

5   Talk into writing   **82**
Susan Jones

Lesson plans for write aloud   100
    Invisible writing   100
    Magic pencil   102
    Paired writing   104
    Talking to a toy   106

6   Talk for reflecting on writing   **108**
Shirley Larkin

Interlude 3   The art of reflection   Corinne Bishop   126

7   Talking about writing – what the children told us   **128**
Ros Fisher

Lesson plans for reflection   144
   Evaluating writing   144
   A step-by-step writing guide   146
   Thinking cap   148
   Two ticks and a wish   150

8   Managing talk for writing in the classroom   **152**
Ros Fisher

Interlude 4   My favourite lesson   Linda Bateman   166

Appendix 1   The research report – talk to text: using talk to
              support writing   168
Appendix 2   Child interview schedule   179

References   181

Index   184

About the authors

Ros Fisher has taught in primary schools in the north-west of England and the USA. She is now Associate Professor in the Graduate School of Education at the University of Exeter. She writes widely about the teaching of literacy and has researched the role of the teacher, and teacher change in current large-scale initiatives to change the teaching of literacy in England. Recent books include *Inside the Literacy Hour* (Routledge, 2002) and an edited collection of papers from an ESRC-funded research seminar series, *Raising Standards in Literacy* (Falmer, 2002). She is currently researching the impact of dialogic talk on young children's understanding of arithmetic.

Susan Jones is a lecturer in education at the University of Exeter, United Kingdom. Her research interests include gender and achievement, classroom interaction and the developing writer. She is the co-author of *Talking, Listening, Learning: Effective Talk in the Primary Classroom* (Open University Press, 2005).

Shirley Larkin has a background in teaching English Literature and in Psychology. She has researched the area of metacognition in young children since 1999. Originally working with Philip Adey on a cognitive acceleration programme in early years science education, she has since explored the role of metacognition in learning to write and in religious education. She has published a number of academic papers in this field and a single-authored book entitled *Metacognition in Young Children* (Routledge, 2010). She currently lectures at the Graduate School of Education, University of Exeter.

Debra Myhill is Professor of Education at the University of Exeter, and is Head of the Graduate School of Education. Her research interests focus principally on aspects of language and literacy teaching, particularly writing and grammar, and talk in the classroom. She is the author of *Better Writers* (Courseware Publications, 2001), co-author of *Talking, Listening, Learning: Effective Talk in the Primary Classroom* (Open University Press, 2005), and co-editor of the *SAGE Handbook of Writing Development* (Sage, 2009).

Anita Wood began her career as a primary school teacher in the London Borough of Tower Hamlets. She now teaches on the Primary PGCE course at the Graduate School of Education at the University of Exeter. Her interests include EAL, drama and children's literature.

Introduction

The talk to text project

The Talk to Text Project developed from an earlier research project in which some members of our current team worked with a group of first schools in West Sussex on classroom talk (see Myhill, Jones and Hopper, 2005). At the end of that project, the headteachers asked if we could continue to work with them on talk but, this time, to focus on talk for writing. Although we knew that a great deal had been written about the importance of using talk to support writing, we also felt that much of this was insufficiently specific. Everyone knew that talk was 'a good thing' when it came to writing but there was very little known about the different ways in which talk supports writing and what happens when children use talk before, during and after writing.

We approached the Esmée Fairbairn Foundation and they agreed to fund the project. Mainly this funding gave us two excellent research fellows who worked closely with the schools. The research was greatly enhanced by the fact that we had one full year as a pilot with the schools that we knew well and then added two more schools from elsewhere in the south of England for the second year when the main study took place. In all, over the period of the project, six schools were involved, with eight teachers, although they were not all with us for the whole project. For the main project we worked with five schools and with six class teachers and their classes of 5, 6 and 7 year-olds.

The project had two main aims. One was to work with the teachers to develop activities that would use talk to support writing and the other was to learn more about what happens when children and teachers talk in this way. We did not want this project to be an 'us and them' project so the teachers were involved throughout. The head teachers helped with writing the research bid. The head teachers and class teachers were involved with the planning and analysis at every stage. Teachers as well as research follows videoed lessons. We held research days when those of us who worked at the university met with those of us who worked in the schools to share ideas. We got together for some of the analysis, and some of the teachers have contributed to this book. The funding from Esmée Fairbairn was particularly helpful in providing supply cover for these meetings to take place.

From the background of previous research and our own knowledge of children and schools, we identified three specific uses for talk to support writing: talk to generate ideas; talk for oral rehearsal; and talk for metacognitive purposes. We felt that each of these purposes required different planning on the part of the teacher and different activities for the children.

In order to clarify these purposes for talk to ourselves, the teachers and the children involved we worked carefully to define exactly what we meant by idea generation, oral rehearsal and metacognition. Following discussions with the

Table I.1   *Framework for using talk to support writing*

Element	Definition	Example	Child speak
Idea generation	This provides children with the opportunity to talk in groups, pairs or with puppets/small world play, etc. about the topic of the writing. It is about the content of their writing.	Role play of a scene from a story, draw a picture and explain it to a partner, talking about own experiences, using artefacts	Getting Ideas
Write aloud	This gives children the chance to put what they want to say into words before they write it. This also means reading their writing aloud after writing to help them 'hear' what their writing sounds like. It is to help with the form of their writing.	Trying out sentences or phrases with a talk partner. Reading invisible writing.	Say it – write it
Reflection	This has two elements: reflection on the process of writing and reflection on the product of writing.	The ending was difficult because I didn't know what to write. I didn't know what to write next and then I remembered my Red Riding Hood story This is a good piece of writing because it is funny.	Thinking about writing

teachers, we changed the terms oral rehearsal to write aloud and metacognition to reflection. In the case of the former this was to distinguish what we wanted to focus on from other forms of oral rehearsal. In the case of the latter it was to use a more easily recognisable term. These definitions and examples can be seen in Table I.1. We also produced a classroom poster depicting a simplified version for children of these Talk to Text elements to be used in the project classrooms. This poster can be seen at the end of the Introduction.

The book

The book is not intended to be merely a research report, although it does contain some discussion of how the project unfolded. Nor is it intended to be just a classroom teaching manual, although it does contain lots of ideas and advice for class teachers. Some chapters contain more of the research and some contain more of the activities but the research and the activities go closely together and support each other. We draw heavily on our data from videos and interviews with children and teachers. This means that both the activities and the theory are illustrated by glimpses from real classrooms and real children.

We are four authors, all of whom were involved in the research project. We have planned the book together and worked together on it. However, we have each taken responsibility for different chapters. So, as is the way with writing, our different voices can be distinguished in the different chapters. But this is not an edited collection with different contributors. It is a self-contained volume with an inner coherence supported by the research that we did together.

In between chapters we also provide various 'interludes'. These are either reflections on the Talk to Text project by teachers who were involved or they are sample lesson plans linked to the three uses of talk described above and set out in Table I.1. These lessons have been planned and written by Anita Wood from the activities developed by the teachers on the project.

The chapters

In the first chapter we provide a theoretical overview of what is currently known about writing and the teaching of writing. This chapter considers research from a variety of perspectives and is the only chapter that is solely theory without any discussion of the classroom practice that is threaded throughout the rest of this book. The poster used in the project classrooms can be found at the end of this Introduction.

In Chapter 2, we give more details about the research project and how it developed. We also give advice and ideas on how you might go about undertaking research in your own classroom. We discuss some of the advantages and pitfalls in conducting research in classrooms. At the end of this chapter, Frances Dunkin, who was head teacher of one of the project schools at the time of the research, reflects on the value she found in being a research active school.

Chapter 3 describes some of the idea generation activities that were used on the project. This is a very practical chapter. Talk to generate ideas is widely used and plenty has already been written about this aspect of talk to support writing. Here we look at the ways in which these children and teachers used talk to help develop the ideas needed for the content of the writing. There is included a lengthy transcript of children talking as they develop their ideas for their writing. This chapter is followed by some sample lesson plans for idea generation.

Chapter 4 explores the idea of 'write aloud'. This use of talk to support writing is new so we explore the theory that underpins this idea as well as its practical implications. This chapter is followed by Rachael Milsom, a teacher on the project, who describes a lesson where she used 'write aloud'.

In Chapter 5 we consider how the talk to generate ideas and write aloud fed into the writing that children produced. We take two lessons and track closely the teacher talk and child talk involved before and during the writing to show in detail the process of composition. This chapter is followed by lesson plans using write aloud.

Chapter 6 examines how children use talk to reflect on their writing. We explore the meaning and value of metacognition and look at how this was developed by children and teachers in the project. This chapter is followed by one of the teachers, Corinne Bishop, describing how she helped children in her class to reflect on the process of writing.

Chapter 7 departs from classroom talk and draws on data from the project to listen to the voices of the children in the project classes. We interviewed six focus children in each of the six classes at the beginning and the end of the year of the main project. These children give us insight into what they think and understand about writing and learning to write. This chapter is followed by the lesson plans for reflection.

The final chapter, Chapter 8, focuses on classroom management for using talk to support writing. Here we draw on what teachers told us and our examination of the video data to bring together ideas about how best to manage the talk. We look closely at some teacher–child interaction and discuss how some forms of interaction support the talk and the writing better than others. This chapter is followed by a final reflection from Linda Bateman, another of the project teachers.

We have also included some more details of the research project in an appendix for those who would like to know more about how we went about data collection and analysis.

Each chapter can be read on its own or as part of the whole. There is some logic to the order but you don't have to read it in the order we chose. We invite you to read the whole book and think about how theory and practice are linked. But we don't mind if you pick and choose the chapters you read. Use the book for your own purposes and we hope you enjoy it.

1 Learning To Write

Debra Myhill

Introduction

Learning to write is one of the most challenging endeavours we offer a young child. We learn to talk naturally and effortlessly through our interactions with others and no child, other than one with specific learning difficulties, does not learn to talk. But learning to write is a taught process and we only learn to write the full repertoire of conventions of our language if we are taught to write, whether that be the demands of shaping letters and spacing words or the demands of conveying meaning through written language. Kress (1994) reminds us that writing is more difficult than reading, because reading is a process of making meaning from text, whereas writing is a process of encoding meaning through text: reading is a receptive process, whereas writing is a productive process. Kellogg (2008) argues that writing is one of the most difficult and demanding intellectual tasks we engage in, and he suggests that it is as intellectually effortful as playing chess. So it is no surprise that children sometimes struggle with writing.

But at the same time, writing is everywhere. In terms of learning to write, it is impossible to separate children's world experiences of reading text from their attempts at writing. As novice writers, they don't enter the writing classroom with no knowledge – they bring a wide understanding of how texts are shaped: understanding of labelling and design on sweet packets; knowing about directions and signposting; being able to discriminate between adverts and stories; knowing the social function of thank you letters, shopping lists, and name labels on property …. These are the foundations upon which learning to write is built. And in the twenty-first-century world of digital natives, young children's experiences of writing are likely to include electronic written forms – emails, text messages, eBay adverts, web pages. Indeed, it would be very easy to argue that, as technology has flourished and children are growing up comfortable with the affordances of technology, young people write more than ever. Certainly, communication that was once oral such as a phone call is increasingly being replaced by texting or emailing, and the accessibility of the internet creates new spaces and provides ease of publishing writing through blogs or wikis, for example. Being able to communicate effectively through writing remains an essential skill for children to learn, not simply because of the role it plays in academic development and assessment, but because of its significance in social development and social networking.

So what can recent research tell us about how children learn to write?

The writing process

Perhaps surprisingly, research in writing is a young and relatively immature field of research, particularly compared with the extensive and well-developed body of research on learning to read. This is particularly true in cognitive psychology where the research has really only developed in the past 30 years or so. But this research has advanced our understanding of the process of writing and of the kinds of demands that writing makes upon our cognitive resources, our 'brain power', you could say.

In the early 1980s, Hayes and Flower (1980) first proposed a model of writing. This was an attempt to explain the mental processes that are involved in moving from ideas in the head to a completed written text on the page or screen. They saw writing as drawing on three important and inter-related components:

- **the writing environment**: this covers everything 'outside the writer's skin that influences the performance of the task' (Hayes and Flower, 1980: 12). So this includes the nature and purpose of the writing task, the writer's motivation to write, and whether it is individual or collaborative writing. You could think of this as the *context* for writing.

- **the writer's long-term memory**: long-term memory is the permanent store of knowledge and experience that we all draw on when we write. This includes our knowledge of texts and text types, our knowledge about writing, and our linguistic knowledge of words and syntax. You could think of this as the principal *resource bank* for writing.

- **the writing process**: this addresses the activities that occur in the period of writing, from the stage of starting to write to the completion of the piece of writing.

Hayes and Flower suggested that the writing process was essentially composed of three different kinds of writing activity. Generating ideas for the writing and working out how you are going to approach the writing task is a *Planning* activity. This might include writing a formal plan but equally it is also simply the thinking and mental planning that often occurs before we attempt to set words on the page. The activity of producing written text, of transforming thoughts or spoken ideas into written language is a *Creating Text* activity. Hayes and Flower called this activity 'translating' but this is perhaps not such a helpful term because of its association with translating from one language to another, and because it suggests that getting words on the page is a simple linear act of translating thoughts into words.

Reading through the text and amending it is a *Reviewing* activity. This may sound vaguely familiar as the National Curriculum talks of writing in terms of Plan – Draft – Revise – Edit. But these are chronological – first you plan, then you draft, etc. However, Hayes and Flower emphasise that planning, writing and reviewing are not simple chronological stages, but they inter-relate and overlap, and that effective writers repeatedly switch between these activities. They argue that we have a monitor, a kind of mental manager, which switches our attention as we are engaged in writing from one activity to another. So as I am creating this text now I am engaged in a Creating Text activity, but I repeatedly stop, sometimes several times a minute, to re-read what I have written. This is a Reviewing activity. And sometimes as I am Creating Text or Reviewing, I think of another point I want to make and I note it down in my plan (I do have a written plan for this!) – this is a Planning activity.

All of this mental activity is influenced by the resources available in the long-term memory and by the writing environment. Many of the pauses while we are Creating Text are while we try to find the right word, searching through the long-term memory for the one that will fit the bill perfectly. Sometimes, pauses during writing are to review whether the developing text matches the task set – for example, does it look like a letter? Is the style of writing appropriate for a letter? And, of course, if you hate writing letters anyway, your motivation to pay attention to your writing may be less than ideal!

For a graphic overview of Hayes and Flower's model see Figure 1.1.

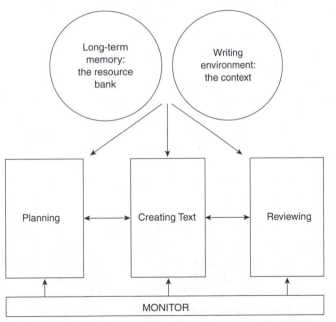

Figure 1.1   A simplified overview of Hayes and Flower's (1980) Model of Writing

But one major problem in Hayes and Flower's model is that it describes writing in proficient writers, writers who no longer need to devote much attention to shaping letters, spelling or punctuation and who approach each new task of writing with a wealth of writing experience behind them. As Berninger et al. (1996) point out, there are significant differences between mature writers and developing writers: 'in skilled writers, planning, translating and revising are mature processes that interact with one another. In beginning and developing writers, each of these processes is still developing and each process is on its own trajectory, developing at its own rate' (1996: 198). We are interested here in early years writers for whom just getting a word onto a page can be a major endeavour.

Creating text: the challenges of orthography and transcription

As any teacher of writing in an early years classroom will know, one of the most significant challenges facing a novice writer is mastering both the physical and the symbolic aspects of writing. Handwriting is a perceptual-motoric skill: in other words, it demands an interplay between fine motor skills and visual perception and evaluation. Learning to control a pencil so that you can shape letters accurately and become a fluent handwriter is a prerequisite skill for developing as a writer. Indeed, recent research (Connelly and Hurst, 2001) has found a direct link between writing fluency and writing quality – children who can write fluently at a good speed tend to write more effective texts. Helping young children to become more fluent writers also supports the activity of creating text (Berninger et al., 2002). There is also evidence (Tucha et al., 2007) that placing too much emphasis upon neatness is a barrier to the development of fluency needed to facilitate growth as a writer. It will probably be no surprise to discover that girls tend to write faster and more fluently than boys (Barnett et al., 2009), though this should not be taken as a deterministic deficit model of boys as writers; boys are not *unavoidably* worse at handwriting than girls. Undoubtedly, a key goal of the teaching of handwriting is to secure fluency and legibility as automated processes, so that the writer is not devoting precious thinking attention to the transcription of text but can instead think more about what they are writing.

Alongside mastering the physical mark-making process of handwriting, young writers are simultaneously learning about the orthographic conventions of written language. Orthography is the way a language represents spoken words in written symbols: the conventions of sound–symbol correspondence and text layout. Research shows that young children's earliest spontaneous writings take the form of *scriptio continua*, strings of letters with no word spaces between them (Ferreiro and Teberosky, 1982). However, children's early mark-making soon shows their sensitivity to the literate world around them and they often produce word-like letter strings. Tolchinsky and Cintas (2001) investigated how early years writers develop understanding of words and word spacing and show that recognising word boundaries is no simple task. Early writers often joined words together or left gaps where there should be none. Our experience as talkers does not help us to understand word boundaries as the word is not as visible in talk as it has to be in writing. I remember as a small child being taught orally the French word for window by my father, and several years later when I started to learn written French at school being very surprised to discover that the word for 'window' was not *lafenêtre* but *la fenêtre*. Young writers have to learn about words as graphemic units, and in English this is not always logical (why *football* but *high chair*?). In the early stages of writing development, lexical and non-lexical items are often amalgamated – for example, *mydog* – the lexical item with its attached grammatical words becomes a unit. This is, of course, exactly what I did as a child learning how to say 'window' in French – I heard the determiner *la* and the noun *fenêtre* as a single word unit. In the Talk to Text project, one noticeable facet of classroom writing was the children's own emphasis on finger-spacing and their reminders to each other to use their fingers to create the spaces between words. These children had learned about the significance of word boundaries.

Too much to do: cognitive overload and working memory

For all of us, child or adult, our working memory (or short-term memory) is critical to our capacity to deal with tasks. In essence, our working memory is that part of the brain which temporarily stores information and allows us to manipulate information to complete a given task (Baddeley and Hitch, 1974). It has limited capacity so if we ask too much of it, we cannot successfully complete the task. Most of us would be able to remember a single telephone number long enough to write it down, but we would struggle to remember two telephone numbers. And the experience that will be familiar to many, of asking for directions and then not being able to recall them all is an example of the limited capacity of our working memory. These, however, are all examples of straightforward retention of information and our ability to recall it. But working memory also deals with manipulating information and if we ask too much of it, it cannot cope: most of us could multiply 2×18 in our heads; far fewer of us could multiply 183×24 because our working memory cannot manage to hold the information required long enough to perform the calculation.

This is called cognitive overload by psychologists and it is particularly relevant to writing because writing is a task which makes heavy demands on our working memory. Young children typically have very small working memory capacities that increase gradually until the teenage years, when adult levels are reached – approximately two to three times greater than that of 4-year-old children (Gathercole et al., 2004). Having to pay attention to handwriting, word spacing and spelling means that young writers have little or no working memory available to think about other aspects of writing, such as what they want to say and how they might say it. Typically, a writer who has progressed beyond *scriptio continua* but is still in the earliest stages of creating text is likely to be concentrating so hard on the letters that make up a word that he or she may not be able to hold a whole sentence in his/her head. McCutcheon (2006: 120) explains that in young children the process of transcription and the process of text generation 'compete for cognitive resources'. This is why it helps writers when they achieve fluent handwriting and when they can spell and punctuate reasonably confidently. It is also why in the Talk to Text project we looked at the ways in which talk might be a tool for reducing cognitive load and releasing working memory capacity to attend to higher-level aspects of writing.

Communities of writers: writing as a social practice

When children learn to write, they are not simply learning to master a symbolic system, they are learning about the social practices that writing embodies. They learn not just to 'do writing', but what writing can do. Learning to write is not simply about learning how to generate written text; it is about learning how to create meaning through text. Some researchers suggest that the urge to make marks on a surface is as instinctive and 'hard-wired' as babbling before learning to reproduce meaningful words and sounds in speech. One study (Gibson and Levin, 1980) demonstrated that if children were given a surface to write on and two tools, only one of which made a mark (e.g. a marker pen and a plastic stick), children rejected the non-marking tool and played with the tool that left a mark. They believed that it was the marks themselves that motivated the children to use the tool that left marks, and that children invested the marks with meaning. It is certainly true that 'if children are provided with marking tools, a suitable surface on which to write, and a safe place to play, they begin to make marks at quite an early age' (Schickendanz and Casbergue, 2004:) and that 'scribbling' is an important aspect of learning to write. Through their early mark-making, children develop some of the hand–eye co-ordination needed for writing, and eventually learn how to discriminate between writing and drawing. Crucially, they also learn that marks can have meaning, be that in terms of pictures or later, words. In the early years, writers do not always understand that the meaning is located in the words and letters on the page; children tend to think the 'writer determines the interpretation of what is written' (Tolchinsky, 2006: 88). So sometimes children will ask an adult what their marks mean.

Of course, for almost all children their first written word is their name. A child's writing of their own name usually shows the highest level of development in emergent writers (Chan, 1998): the shaping of letters, the sequencing of letters in the name, and the understanding of the concept of a word are often evident in a child's writing of his/her name before they are evident more generally in their writing. A child's name is highly meaningful in terms of his/her identity and social relationships. A child learns that writing your name on possessions can identify something as belonging to you, writing your name on a birthday card can enable you to send a greeting to someone who is not present, that writing your surname can inform people of which family you belong to. This is social knowledge of the power of written text in getting things done.

Home and school literacy experiences

All of this means, as we noted in the introduction, that young children come to school with existing knowledge and understanding of writing, drawn from their own literacy experiences in the home and in the world around them. And, of course, one challenge for teachers of writing is that these literacy experiences are very varied. Almost all children will see adults in the home writing, whether texting friends or leaving a note to the milkman. However, some children have writing experiences that are more like the sort of writing that happens in school. They will have made birthday cards and written messages in them, for example, and others will not. Some will have adults who have written with them or for them, and others will not. Some of these experiences are helpful in how they get on in school and others are not. These latter experiences are sometimes unrecognised or ignored by their teachers. The pathway by which children become confident writers is different for different children and they bring with them to the classroom what Garton and Pratt (1989) called a 'network of understandings' about writing.

One element of this network of understanding relates to children's understanding of text. Kress (1997) used his own daughter's writing as the basis for exploring how early writing developed and his work emphasises the interrelationship of the written word and the visual in early attempts at writing. He maintains that children's early attempts at writing are fundamentally about design, about constructing meaning from the available resources, making early writing active and transformative, not simply imitative. This idea that learning to write is much more than imitation is a point also made by Ferreiro and Teberosky (1982) who suggest that children generate their own theories about writing, such as the child who made her writing taller for people who were bigger! Kress argues that children as young as 4 have an understanding of genre, and gives examples of children writing newspapers with many of the genre features evident. This knowledge of genre and text derives from out-of-school encounters and includes the impact of new technologies on the way meanings are communicated in text. A project by the Qualifications and Curriculum Authority (QCA) and the United Kingdom Literacy Association (UKLA) focused upon the way early writing is a sophisticated blend of the visual and the verbal, reflecting children's social experiences of text. They note that:

> new forms of communication, and the knowledge of texts brought to the classroom by even the very youngest readers and writers, pose new questions for teaching and learning. Many books and other media now available in schools cannot be read by attention to writing alone. (QCA/UKLA, 2004: 5)

Their work highlights how contemporary texts, both those found in school and out of school, use features such as 'layout, font size and shape and colour to add to the information or stories contained in the words' and that these texts additionally 'make use of spatial arrangements to convey ideas' (QCA/UKLA, 2004: 5). Kress (1997) feels that, in the planning and teaching of writing, we do not take sufficient account of this inter-relationship of the visual and the verbal and that we tend to ignore the way the 'page' is 'a meaningful or significant element in writing' (Kress, 1997: 86). Many teachers would suggest that this is because the assessment framework in the National Curriculum gives no credit for children's use of the visual and spatial aspects of writing.

Many researchers have highlighted the discontinuities between writing at home and at school. Nixon and Topping (2001: 44) summarise this succinctly by suggesting that 'before school, emergent writing tends to be social and functional; in school, it risks becoming socially isolated and largely purposeless'. Certainly, for children who come from home backgrounds in which there has been a wide range of literacy experience, the experience of writing tends to move from a very social, interactive and exploratory process, characterised by a high level of one-to-one engagement, to one which is more likely to be focused on direct instruction and routinised activities. The creation of writing environments in classrooms which embed writing in play and allow children to generate authentic contexts for writing, and playing with writing, helps to avoid some of these discontinuities between home and school.

The classroom as a writing community

Creating a classroom which is conducive to the learning of writing is essentially about developing a writing community which allows for high levels of exploration, experimentation and talk within the context of sensitively structured teaching input. Socio-constructivist research on writing suggests that there are three pedagogical principles (Englert et al., 2006: 209) which should inform the teaching of writing:

- **Sociocognitive apprenticeships**: this involves working alongside more competent writers to learn more about writing, and might include familiar activities such as the teacher acting as scribe or teacher modelling of a writing activity.

- **Procedural facilitation and tools**: this involves supporting the cognitive process of writing with steps or strategies that help children become independent writers. This could range from simple mnemonics to remember spellings to writing frames which give structural prompts for connecting paragraphs or structured peer assessment.

- **Participation in communities of practice**: this involves developing shared knowledge and understanding of writing and participatory ways of working, and would include activities such as collaborative writing, and classrooms which foster a rich talk environment for writing activities.

It is easy to see how many of the activities which are now common in many classrooms fit with these three principles. In recent years, primary classrooms have become familiar with strategies for teaching writing which include the shared construction of text, the use of models, guided writing, and offering children frames or prompts for writing. Below are three case studies which exemplify these principles in practice and which indicate the benefits these ways of working offer young writers.

Case Study 1: Sociocognitive Apprenticeships

The LEAP Project (Literacy Environments for Accelerated Progress)

This project took place in the USA and focused on establishing a year-long apprenticeship approach to writing. Two teachers sharing an early years classroom with many struggling writers participated in the project, which emphasized creating ways of teaching which helped students to participate actively in writing and which used modelling and scaffolding as methods of support. The project also tried to create a community of practice which acknowledged children as individuals with cultural backgrounds of their own. Throughout the project, the teachers modelled writing and verbalized their thinking about writing. Specific writing practices which they introduced included: writing topic sentences; transforming ideas into detail sentences; underlining topic sentences; indenting by pushing over the beginning of the paragraph using arrows; using invented spellings; sounding out words; providing spaces between words; helping partners to write sentences; and using capital letters and full stops.

The project was successful in supporting children's writing development. The project leaders claim that 'In these supported contexts, children seem "enabled" as writers rather than "disabled" and have the potential to exercise higher order thinking and to participate in executive tasks that might normally be relegated to only the most academically advanced learners in the classroom'. For example, two boys in the project, Desmond and Joseph, who began the course at an emergent literacy stage and were identified as in need of language support, made significant gains in reading and writing competence and no longer required additional support.

Englert, C.S., Berry, R. and Dunsmore, K. (2001) 'Case Study of the Apprenticeship Process: Another Perspective on the Apprentice and the Scaffolding Metaphor', *Journal of Learning Disabilities,* 34(2): 152–71.

Case Study 2: Procedural Tools and Facilitation

Emergent writing: the impact of structured peer interaction

This project paired together younger Year 1 children with older Year 6 children in a Paired Writing activity. The peer interaction was structured in order to help the children work together collaboratively over a period of six weeks. The structure provided was a series of metacognitive prompts which focused thinking on the relevant stage of writing, such as planning, drafting or editing. In the 'ideas generation' stage, for example, a series of questions were provided for the older writers to ask the younger writers to help them generate ideas.

The children who had been involved in the collaborative writing with structured peer interaction improved their writing significantly more than the other children. In addition, they had grown in confidence and developed more positive attitudes to writing, including greater willingness to write and to share their writing with others. An important 'side-effect' was that many of the young children formed close relationships with their older peer tutor.

Nixon, J.G. and Topping, K.J (2001) Emergent Writing: the Impact of Structured Peer Assessment, *Educational Psychology*, 21 (1) 42–55

Case Study 3: Participation in Communities of Practice

This project involved a multi-age primary classroom in an urban school in Southern California. The class was led by two teachers whose goal was to create a collaborative writing community which also fostered independence and self-regulation. They adopted the writing workshop approach and gave children freedom to choose materials and work partners, topics to write about, and freedom to move around the room. The two teachers worked with individuals and partnerships giving guidance and some direct instruction. This combination of freedom and guidance enabled these young writers to create meaningful texts which expressed their own identities and voice. The children created worlds in writing which reflected or shaped what these writers felt the world was or should be like. The authors argue that the collaborative community approach helped these children to find their writing voice and to construct their own identities.

Capello, M. (2006) 'Under Construction: Voice and Identity Development in Writing Workshop', *Language Arts*, 83(6): 482.

Ways with words: language development in writing

Becoming a writer means extending your language repertoire from spoken forms to written forms and learning how to express yourself using the syntactical structures appropriate to writing. Kress (1994) suggests that one of the most significant features of language development in young writers is learning about the sentence. The sentence does not really exist in speech – we talk mostly in broken sentences, fragments, hesitations and repetitions which are more accurately called utterances rather than sentences. But the sentence is the building-block of writing. Sentences have to express ideas in a much more 'rule-bound' way than spoken utterances, and sentences in a text have to connect with each other in a more coherent and logical manner than is necessary in talk. Kress argues that very young writers treat the sentence as a textual unit rather than a syntactical unit: think of the way very young writers' first texts are single sentences. In the early stages of learning to write, they also often tend to see the sentence as synonymous with the line – you may well know young writers whose writing gets smaller and smaller as they get nearer to the end of the line in order to fit it in.

Young writers' language does tend to develop along broadly similar trajectories as they gain experience and confidence in writing. There have been several studies of children's language development in writing, though none of these has looked in a thorough way at language development from beginning to write through to being able to write with some accomplishment. It is curious that there is a vast body of research and understanding about how children learn to talk but by comparison very little about the parallel developmental pattern in writing. The most substantial study in England was conducted by Katharine Perera, looking at primary writers. She argued that it is important for teachers to have 'some understanding of the stages that children pass through in their development as writers' (1984: 2) and to understand some of the challenges young writers face in mastering the demands of writing. This is not so that teachers can give grammar lessons on areas of weakness, but so that teachers can recognise linguistic development which might be obscured by the more surface problems in handwriting, spelling or punctuation. It is one way to see signs of growth. Table 1.1 on p. 12 summarises some of the developmental features identified by Perera (1984).

Although this pattern of development appears to be about grammatical development, in fact it reflects both the writer's growing ability to understand the needs of a particular text or a particular audience, and the way they are beginning to grapple with how written language expresses complex ideas. Perera notes how the passive voice is difficult for young writers to understand, not because the grammar is hard but because the way a passive voice changes meaning is hard. When common sense experience can be used there is no problem – so 'The dog ate the bone' re-shaped as a passive ('The bone was eaten by the dog') tends to be

Table 1.1   Summary of pattern of language development in writing (Perera, 1984)

Feature	Development patterns
Clauses/sentences	Clauses and sentences get longer.
Noun phrases	Simple noun phrases as novice writers (*a hungry bear*), moving to longer noun phrases with more complex structures (e.g. *a hungry bear with a rumbly tummy*).
Verb phrases	Simple active verbs only in early writing, moving to being able to use passives and modals (*could; should; would*, etc.).
Complex sentences	Moving from using a lot of co-ordination (*and/but*) to using more subordinate clauses and then to a wider variety of subordinate clause types.
Adverbial clauses	Use of time adverbials most frequently, probably linked with chronological writing (e.g. *yesterday; then; later; after that*, etc.).
Cohesion	Use of reference, substitution and ellipsis is not mastered quickly and young writers often have repetitive texts.
Sentence/clause starts	Young writers often use the same pronoun repeatedly in subject position at the start of a sentence or clause (e.g. *I went home and I had tea and I ate too many sausages and I was sick.*)
Paragraphs	Initially sentences make sense on their own as units but do not relate well to other sentences; as writers develop they become better at linking sentences into a paragraph and whole text.

understood because children know dogs eat bones not vice versa. But when the subject and object are equally plausible as 'do-ers' of the action, children tend to give priority to word order and would find it hard to grasp that 'Jane attacked Sarah' represents the same action as 'Sarah was attacked by Jane'. Perera also noted that, whilst young writers have no problems with time-related connectives (e.g. *then, finally, later*) children struggle with causal and adversative connectives, such as: *on the other hand*; *as a result*; *for this reason*; and *in contrast*. This is likely to be because these connectives express complex relationships between ideas and arguments. As children's *thinking* develops, so does their writing.

Language development: a social process

Language development in writing is predominantly a social process, heavily influenced by children's home and school experiences of talk, but also by their growing encounters with texts, both as producers of text and consumers of texts. Reading and writing help children to become readers and writers. This view of language development, as heavily influenced by our social engagement with communication as language users, contrasts with notions of language development as innate. For many years, researchers, led by the then seminal work of Noam Chomsky, believed that as humans we are 'hard-wired' for language and that 'infants are born with initial innate theories, and that they begin revising these theories even in infancy itself' (Gopnik, 2003: 241). But now these views of language learning are generally rejected in favour of an understanding that, while the capacity to learn language may be a natural predisposition, its trajectory of development is shaped only by meaningful social interactions with others.

For young writers, a significant social development which interacts with language development in writing is being able to write for a reader, rather than wholly for oneself. Perera (1987) described this as moving from writing for self to writing for others. She suggested that language development in writing, including the syntactical structures evident, reflects young writers' growing facility to meet the needs of a reader. So, for example, the developmental pattern of lengthening noun phrases tends to be a sign that the writer is providing more detail for a reader, and the use of causal connectives indicates a clearer expression of argument. The linguistic and the social march hand-in-hand in writing development. Flower (1979) described this developmental trajectory as the move from Writer-based prose to Reader-based prose. Reader-based prose, she maintains, 'creates a shared language and shared context between writer and reader … Good writing, therefore, is the cognitively demanding transformation of the natural but private expressions of Writer-Based thought into a structure and style adapted to a reader' (Flower, 1979: 20). This development mirrors the movement in learning to talk from monologic talk to genuine dialogue where interaction creates shared communication. This monologic talk is, of course, what Piaget described as egocentricity or private speech in which children voice their thoughts aloud as they have not yet learned to control their thoughts internally. Young writers are essentially monologic writers, and they assume the reader understands what they are trying to communicate. As children mature, they become more confident shaping text with readers in mind, although sophisticated mastery of the reader–writer relationship remains a problem even in the secondary school (and beyond!). However, this does not mean that young writers are only capable of monologic writing: one boy, Frankie, in our research project, wrote the text below after a visit by Val Biro to the classroom, talking about the *Gumdrop* stories. Frankie is creating his own *Gumdrop* story, and the emerging relationship with a reader is evident: he positions his readers with adjectives (*amazing; cheeky*) to share his viewpoint; he directly addresses his readership (*if you look closely …*), and he sets up a potential threat, or narrative problem, by linking the escaped rhino with the familiar characters of the *Gumdrop* stories (Gumdrop, Mr Oldcastle and Black Horace).

> This is the nisy amazing longleat. There are some very cheeky monkeys there. If you look closely you mite see some juicy fruit and a grey rhino. Because it has ascaped. I hope he dosent see gumdrop or mr old castele or Black Horace.

Talk to text

We have already noted the importance of young writers mastering the differing demands of spoken and written forms. The differences between talk and writing are significant, though as mature speakers and writers we often take these differences for granted. In all languages, there are distinctions between the conventions and the possibilities of talk and those of writing, and in some the differences are far stronger than in English. Arabic children have to learn to write a form of Arabic which they do not hear spoken; and they speak a colloquial form of Arabic which they never see written. In English, the differences between speech and writing are less pronounced, though of course their similarity may make it harder for children to make the distinction.

One very obvious difference between talk and writing is that talk is of the moment, whereas writing creates a record which can be stored permanently. Once someone has spoken, unless it has been recorded artificially, that talk cannot be re-heard, which means that when we talk we tend to help our listeners by giving them key information first so that they have cues about what is coming next. A written text can be retained and re-read if necessary. Talk always occurs in a context and is often deeply embedded in that context: it is a context which is shared with the listener so the talker does not need to make an effort to be explicit and clarify things. So talk can use words like 'there' and 'that one' with no need of further elaboration. In contrast, writing is context-free and is likely to be read in a different context from that in which it was written (possibly hundreds of years later) and so it has to help the reader by clarifying and explaining more carefully. As a speaker you get instant feedback on how your talk is being received – either through direct responses such as questions or comments, or through non-verbal feedback such as nods, smiles or expressions of puzzlement. But as a writer, feedback is either delayed or does not happen at all, so as we write we have to imagine our reader and their possible responses. This links back to the challenges that young writers have in writing for a reader, discussed in the previous section.

Because talk occurs in a live context with at least two people participating, it is able to do things which writing cannot do. Features of talk, such as intonation, stress, volume, pitch and pausing all create possibilities for signalling how the talk should be heard. These features can convey excitement, surprise, disappointment, and, most importantly, they give the listener strong support in recognising what is the most important word or idea. Kress (1994) argued that intonation in speech was equivalent to emphasis in writing. Moreover, talk is usually accompanied by a whole battery of non-verbal communication, both facial and body language, which provides further support for the listener's interpretation. In writing, the only way the writer can achieve similar effects is through vocabulary and imagery choices and through varying the syntactical structure of the sentence. This poses a real challenge, not just for young writers but for writers of all ages. There are, of course, things writing can do that talk cannot do: the visual nature of writing can exploit font, colour, layout and typographic features such as emboldening or italicisation to support the shaping of meaning. Young writers often know about the graphic potential of writing: for example, think of young writers who capitalise and use a string of exclamation marks for emphasis ('GO AWAY!!!!!').

Linguistically, too, talk is very different from writing and writing is not talk written down. A quick glance at any transcription of talk makes it very clear how untidy talk is and how reliant it is on a shared context. The extract below is taken from a research interview in one of our research projects and it makes very clear how different talk is from writing. The shared context of a lesson just observed underlies the exchange; there are no grammatically complete sentences, and the utterances are full of hesitations and fillers (like 'umm') and incomplete fragments. Both speakers support each other in sustaining the conversation through the OKs and 'yeah'.

Interviewer	… so, what I just want you to do is just reflect on the lesson that you've just done …
Teacher	OK
Interviewer	… and think about, umm, how you think it went in terms of the children's learning, and, your assessment of what they learned …
Teacher	mmm …
Interviewer	and how, did things go according to plan, anything like that.
Teacher	OK
Interviewer	… really, just reflecting on it
Teacher	umm, I think, ooh, actually one of the things I noticed when we were, I think what I should've done, umm, after the start of it so you said here like, sort of talk about, how we're now gonna focus in on word level rather than …
Interviewer	yeah
Teacher	text level.

In talk, we also tend to link ideas together in a linear way, often using connectives such as 'and', 'but' or 'so', because this is easier for a listener to follow than hierarchical relationships, such as those created by connectives such as 'unless', 'since' or 'although'. Because talk occurs in time, it often has more chronological, time-related connectives whereas writing makes use of a broader range of connectives. Sentence structure varies too, with more subordination and more sentences which start with something other than the subject, such as an adverbial (e.g. *That evening*) or a non-finite clause (e.g. *Raising his hand, he …*). These differences reflect 'writerly' patterns of expression and young writers have few models for these in their spoken interactions. Table 1.2 summarises some of these differences.

Table 1.2   Summary of some of the key differences between speaking and writing

Talk	Writing
ephemeral	permanent
context-bound	context-free
reliant on phonic representation	reliant on graphic representation
occurs in time	occurs in space
instant feedback	delayed or no feedback
utterances	sentences
linear connections (e.g. *and*)	hierarchical connections (e.g. *because; unless*)
syntactically fragmented	syntactically complete
more grammatical words (prepositions, conjunctions, determiners)	more meaning words (nouns, verbs, adjectives and adverbs)
more co-ordination	more subordination
fewer non-finite clauses	more non-finite clauses
fewer adjectives	more adjectives
more simple noun phrases	longer noun phrases
more active verbs	more passive verbs

The influence of talk on writing

Given these differences between talking and writing, it is not surprising that this is a challenge for young and developing writers. Bereiter and Scardamalia (1982) described this challenge as the problem of switching from oral to graphic expression, and moving from talking to a speaker who is present to writing for an unknown reader. However, there is evidence that children learn fairly quickly in their primary years that 'writing is not simply the language of speech written down' (Perera, 1987: 17). Her research with older primary children found that, by the age of 8, there was very little evidence of oral constructions in children's writing, and she concludes that 'as young as eight … children are differentiating the written from the spoken language and are not simply writing down what they would say' (Perera, 1986: 96). The oral constructions she investigated represented structures which are very typical in speech but which never occur in writing: this includes constructions such as vague completers, like 'or something' and 'stuff like that'; the pattern of recapitulating the pronoun ('My nan, she ...') and the generalised, indefinite use of this/these as in 'there was this man'. Her study suggests that developmentally children's ability to discriminate language distinctions between speech and writing increases with age: 'on the one hand, as they get older they use in their writing grammatical constructions that are more advanced than those they use in speech; on the other hand, they use in their speech an increasing proportion of specifically oral constructions' (1986: 91).

However, although children do learn not to write in exactly the way they speak, the influence of speech patterns on writing remains significant, not just for young writers but right through secondary school. Using GCSE English examination scripts as the data source, Massey et al. (2005) reported that many students were using non-Standard and colloquial forms in their writing which were drawn from their oral repertoire. Myhill (2009a) found that writing development in the secondary phase is marked in part by the growing ability to move away from replicating speech patterns in writing and towards adopting more 'writerly' forms – for example, by not always starting a sentence with the subject or by using occasional short sentences or verbless sentences for effect. This need to become increasingly adept at re-shaping spoken forms into writing forms is compounded by the child's social background. Perera (1984) observed that a differential gap between speech and writing exists for different language users: 'although all children have to alter their language significantly as they move from casual speech to formal writing, those whose oral language differs markedly from Standard English will have a particularly demanding adjustment to make' (1984: 213). Middle-class first language speakers are advantaged from the outset. Kress notes that:

> the structure of the spoken form of their [middle class] dialects is very strongly influenced by the structures of writing. As a result, the difference between the syntax of speech and that of writing is far less for such groups than it is for groups whose dialects are little if at all influenced by the structure of writing. (1994: 5)

In other words, the typical speech patterns of children from middle-class families are closer to the patterns of writing and so these children have less of a gap to bridge between oral and written language. Such talk in the home also tends to introduce children to a wider range of vocabulary (Lareau, 2003) giving them a broader and richer word pool on which to draw in their writing. Indeed, Lareau's naturalistic observations of children at home and at school revealed important differences in language and child-rearing styles between the different home backgrounds. Hasan (2002) argues that the way language is used in some homes fits better with the expectations of language use in school. Lareau claims that this privileges the children of middle-class families as they are more likely to fit into school language practices. She concludes, 'It is the ways that institutions function that ends up conveying advantage to middle-class children' (2003: 160).

The importance of talk in supporting early writing

James Britton (1970: 29) famously described writing as floating 'on a sea of talk', and it has become almost commonplace to advocate the importance of talk in the writing classroom. There is a strong body of research which records the social nature of the talk experience, and how the talk which surrounds the process of writing is rich with social understandings, negotiations and the building of identity. Dyson (2002) illustrates how one child, Denise, uses talk as she writes to sustain her relationships with the friends around her and with the teacher, including discussions with a friend about how big the writing should be and with the teacher about how her talk is disturbing others. Our own Talk to Text project was full of these kinds of interactions. Some of the interactions are related to managing getting the task done: one girl tells her partner 'You have to write that down', whilst another girl prompts her partner to get on with task – 'Come on, Robert ...' Other interactions focus more closely on the process of writing, as the young writers make visible their thinking processes to each other – 'I've thought of my sentence' – or support each other with the writing process – 'Why don't you come up with another idea?'. The writers frequently vocalised their writing aloud as they wrote, sounded out spellings, and evaluated what they had done to themselves ('Yes, that's OK'). Dyson describes this kind of talk as social dialogue which invites children 'into the literate activities of classroom worlds' (Dyson, 2002: 62).

However, the precise relationship between talk and writing and how teaching supports the transition from talk to text is significantly under-researched. We do know that oral development is linked with writing development, and that children who are more proficient speakers are also better writers. But we don't know whether teaching interventions which target developing a child's oral language impacts upon their writing achievement (Shanahan, 2006: 174) even if intuitively we may feel it must. From a New Zealand perspective, Parr, Jesson and McNaughton (2009) have investigated some of these relationships between talk and writing in the context of their national primary literacy curriculum. Like others, they note the way in which talk is often used as the basis for developing content for writing, particularly drawing on a child's personal experiences. Here talk is generative, supporting the development and articulation of ideas for writing prior to the act of transforming those ideas into written text. Like Dyson, they also note the importance of the joint interactions around the writing of a text, though they place more emphasis on these interactions as scaffolding interactions where the novice writer is supported by a more expert peer or adult. Parr et al. have a third category of talk which they term 'inter-textual talk' (2009: 254) which is more directly focused upon 'explicit guidance ... enabling children to develop more control and awareness in their writing' (2009: 255). This explicit guidance addresses inter-textual links between reading and writing, illustrates structural and linguistic aspects of writing, and highlights the process of writing. They suggest that this use of talk to support writing is under-utilised but conclude by noting the dearth of 'deliberate systematic investigation of the assumed significance of talk to writing' (2009: 257).

This is where our own Talk to Text project begins. We have come a long way since the late 1980s when Christie (1987) criticised how teachers used talk in the classroom to support early years writers in moving from spoken to written forms. She argued that the way teachers talked in preparation for writing was insufficiently challenging and did not extend either children's thinking or help young writers to access the more writerly forms that they needed. Many of the pedagogical strategies adopted in the National Literacy Strategy/Primary National Strategy have given teachers much greater opportunities for supporting the movement from talk to text and for providing challenging oral interactions around text. Shared composition, for example, makes visible how text grows from spoken ideas, teacher modelling makes visible some of the thinking which underpins this transition, and guided writing provides more focused support for groups of writers in crossing the bridge from talk to text. But the sparsity of research which explores how this works in practice motivated us to embark on the Talk to Text project, working with teachers to investigate how talk becomes text.

2 Exploring Classroom Talk Through Action Research

Susan Jones

Introduction

This book is not just a book about a research project. It aims to explore classroom practice in the use of talk to support young children as they learn to write. But before we start to look into the classrooms and what teachers and children are doing in their writing lessons, we want to consider the part that teachers can play in any research project. Many books have been written by authors who commentate on classroom practice and on research projects conducted in classrooms. An essential part of this book is that it draws on the authors' knowledge of classrooms from both teaching and research perspectives. The project was set up for us, as researchers and teachers, to work together to find out more about the relationship between talk and writing. Much of the research described in the previous chapter was conducted by researchers going in and trying out ideas. In the Talk to Text Project the teachers were essential members of the research team. They listened to our ideas, gleaned largely from the research literature, and added their own ideas, developed through many years' experience. The outcome was most rewarding for researchers, teachers and the schools as a whole.

This chapter aims to briefly outline the project, then to take some of what we have learned from working with teachers on action research projects, both the Talk to Text project and others, and offer some practical suggestions for how you might employ research techniques to facilitate your own reflective practice, whether exploring habitual practice and raising questions about this or what happens when you make a conscious effort to change what you do and introduce new or experimental approaches into your own teaching.

The teachers involved in the Talk to Text project were recruited as part of a research study knowing they would be asked to implement strategies designed by the research team to explore how different talk activities might support writing.

They knew their own use, development and evaluation of the strategies would be a crucial part of the project given that no strategy looks exactly the same in any two classrooms and that how and why certain activities worked or didn't in different contexts would be important in interpreting the findings. As such, the project stood within the action research tradition in which the teacher is not seen merely as the subject of research principally undertaken by others in order to inform teachers how to teach, but rather the teacher is actively engaged in critically commenting on the research process, findings and any subsequent implications for practice. Educational research undertaken as a purely academic endeavour by professional researchers might well be viewed by teachers as 'ivory towered' and somewhat removed from the experiences of those who do the job day in, day out. A particular feature of action research in the classroom is the opportunity it offers for teachers to scrutinise and reflect on their own practice, take ownership of problems and potential solutions and to engage in informed discussion within a community of practice. Thus action research has the potential to enable teachers to 'look beyond their classrooms for evidence and think rigorously about their practice' (OECD, 2002) or create a climate in which they can become 'critically intelligent' (Prestage et al., 2003). As a collaborative project between Exeter University and primary schools drawn from two different Local Education Authorities the project sought to exploit the advantages of this partnership by giving full weight to the teacher as the expert in the classroom, within the context of a formal research project; thus allowing the expertise of academic researchers to inform and be informed by professional insight.

An outline of the project

The key aims and purposes of the Talk to Text project were to investigate how creating explicit opportunities for talk can enhance children's early attempts at writing, and to develop practical and successful ways of introducing talk-for-writing activities into the classroom. Writing is one of the most complex cognitive activities that primary children undertake: it requires the motor skills to form letters and words, the oral and cognitive skills to match a phonetic sound to a written letter and then to build these letters into words conforming to conventional spelling, and the ability to translate spoken language into written forms, as well as linguistic knowledge about sentence formation, punctuation and grammar. As writers develop and some skills become automated they require the skill to evaluate what they have written in terms of how it meets the demands of the set task and how it might impact on the reader. If talk is to address the complexity of this task then it is not just talk per se, but the strategic use of different kinds of talk that is likely to act as a support for young writers. To this end the intervention activities focused around three key strategic elements in the writing process, the original identifiers for these elements were:

- Idea generation – What shall I write?

  o Talking about the content of writing, separate from the act of writing

- Oral rehearsal – How shall I write it?

  o Translating spoken ideas into written sentences orally just before they are written

- Metacognition – How do I write?

  o Talking about thinking processes during writing.

Activities were initially developed by the research team, although the schools were encouraged to shape the activities to suit the classroom context. Our expectations were that teachers would be comfortable with idea generation activities but that oral rehearsal and the metacognitive activities would be less familiar. Indeed visiting the research literature revealed that the term oral rehearsal was being used in different ways within the research community, and these interpretations were also at variance with our own understanding. As a consequence we produced a working definition of the terms for our own benefit as well for the teachers. By the end of the pilot phase of the project we had changed our terminology for the key elements, referring to:

- Idea generation (see Chapter 3)

- Write aloud (see Chapter 4)

- Reflection (see Chapter 6)

We also produced a child-friendly version displayed on classroom posters.

- Getting ideas

- Say it – write it

- Thinking about writing

The detailed pilot also highlighted that a critical moment for the children involved was precisely the point at which they moved from talking to text making. Many of the pilot observation schedules recorded that however responsive the children have been in the idea generation activities, and however successful these activities may appear to have been in generating ideas or engagement, often the act of picking up the pencil removed the child from the creativity of the oral activity to the practicality of writing. Older habits and routines seemed to be well embedded in their writing behaviour, habits that focused on the surface features of the text such as spelling and handwriting, and as soon as the act of writing began these habitual practices predominated. Enabling children to take what they had generated in the talk activities into their writing behaviour was identified as a key moment in terms of the efficacy of the intervention activities. Thus it was this interface between the two media of talking and writing that became the main focus of the research and in exploring not only how talk might support writing but also how this operates differently at different points in the writing process within the classroom. Analysing this talk, the move from talk to text and how the talk activities impacted on the texts produced, is explored in Chapter 5.

The project involved six classes drawn from five primary schools in two geographical regions of the south west of England. All the classes were either Year 1 or Year 2 or mixed classes of both year groups. Hence we were working with very young writers, some at the very beginning of their development as writers. For comparison purposes we also recruited two further schools, one from each region, who were not implementing the talk activities. The comparison group was not conceived with the intention of demonstrating improvement in the writing from the project schools. It is difficult to demonstrate improvement that is independent of demographic influences, teacher and school effects, even with very large samples, but we were able to observe changing classroom climates as a result of increasing talk-based activities in the project schools. Within each class we selected six focus children for detailed observation: one boy and one girl were drawn from three achievement groups: high, average and low. Thus we were able to explore how engaging in talk and producing texts might operate differentially by either gender or achievement.

Throughout the project, teachers captured writing lessons on video. Once a term the research team visited each school and conducted a formal observation during a videoed lesson. The videos captured the initial whole-class set up of the writing task and final plenary plus two of the focus children talking and writing in pairs at tables. These pairs always involved a boy and a girl matched for achievement. The writing from these lessons was also collected for analysis. At the beginning and end of the project we collected a matched sample of writing from all the schools in the project – the project group and the comparison group. We also interviewed focus children from both groups of schools at the beginning and end of the project about their attitudes to writing and this is discussed in Chapter 7. Throughout the project we met with teachers and discussed their ideas of how the project was going. These days were important as they ensured that the project was fully collaborative between the university and the schools.

Thus the data collected for the project included:

- Video recordings
- Classroom observations
- Examples of children's writing
- Interviews with children.

Each of these methods will be discussed in turn in terms of how you might make use of these techniques to explore your own practice.

The video data

The idea of allowing a video camera to capture one's own teaching would probably be alarming to most teachers. Despite a very natural anxiety about teaching in front of the camera, and a clear embarrassment factor at subsequently watching themselves teach, teachers who have used this means of exploring their own practice, have concluded that what they learn from it more than compensates for the initial discomfort. In both the Talk to Text project and previous action research projects conducted by members of the team, cameras were originally introduced as a means of collecting research data but were subsequently viewed by the teachers as a means of informing their own practice. In the context of the Talk to Text project, however, we were as interested in the interactions between children as those between the teacher and the child and video data is especially useful in capturing the interactions between children that often go unobserved or unheard in our classrooms. Observing children talking and working together not only informs us of how different strategies and activities support learning, but also reveals misunderstandings and student perspectives on what is being learnt and why. Thus the video camera can reveal our own use of talk as teachers and how this impacts on learning, as well as children's talk which tells us something about what is being learned. In the Talk to Text project the cameras tended to be left in the classrooms whether they were being used or not, thus familiarising the children with having the cameras around so they were never really sure whether they were in use or not.

Classroom interactions are complex and interconnected, in real time teachers respond moment by moment to occurrences and questions based on their professional understanding of the curriculum and the children in their class. A clear danger in slowing this interaction down and revisiting it is the ample opportunity it presents for teachers to observe every verbal tick, every poorly phrased question, every hasty decision, indeed all the normal everyday behaviour that defines the social context of the classroom and the teachers' place in it. If all that a video camera reveals is the obvious conclusion that we all could do better – then it would be a pointless and soul-destroying activity. It is important, therefore, to be clear what you want to know before you begin recording so that this becomes the focus of your attention when you play it back. Table 2.1 offers some suggestions for questions you might ask, this is not meant to be an exhaustive list nor are the implications definitive in any way, the purpose here is to show the cyclical nature of the approach as outlined in Figure 2.1.

Subsequent chapters in this book may give you some ideas for strategically employing certain talk activities to support writing. You can then discover for yourself the impact of these strategies on what happens in the classroom.

The decision to reflect on practice in this way is quite a commitment, not so much in recording the lessons but in the time taken to reflect on what you see. Having a clear focus should help make the process more manageable – you are not interested in everything you do, only in small details. Clearly this kind of

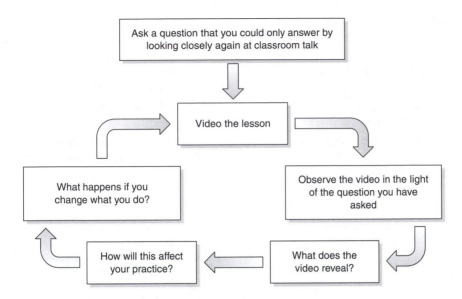

Figure 2.1   The cycle of investigating classroom practice

Table 2.1   Questions addressed by video observation

Teacher/Child talk	Implications
1. In whole-class sessions what is the balance between the amount of talking I do and the amount of talking the children do?	1. Do I need to change this pattern – how?
2. How many different children speak?	2. How can I increase participation levels for certain children?
3. Trying out and comparing different talk activities OR comparing group talk with paired talk: • Who talks? • What do they talk about? • What do they find difficult?	3. What already works well with this class? Which activities/groupings work best? Do they need more support with some talk activities?
4. What do I do with children's misunderstandings?	4. Do children feel comfortable 'being wrong' – can I make 'being wrong' a normal part of talking and learning?

(Continued)

Table 2.1 (Continued)

Child/Child talk	Implications
1. Are there examples of misunderstanding?	1. Does this need whole-class or individual support?
2. What do children think is important about the task?	2. Where do these ideas come from?
3. Trying out and comparing different talk activities: • Who talks most? • What do they talk about? • What do they find difficult?	3. Should I change work partners? Should I alter/adapt the activities?
4. What happens if I have mixed ability pairings?	4. What is gained and lost by this approach? When might I use it?

approach works best as a whole-school initiative such that good practice can be shared and common concerns addressed. Within the research projects our teachers found that it was talking with other teachers about what they had learned about their own practice that gave value to the experience. Discovering shared issues and discussing possible implications and outcomes helped establish the notion of a community of practice in which teachers were the experts in addressing issues of pedagogy within the school. Within the context of the research project, the research process was revealing things these teachers were beginning to discover for themselves, and this made the findings feel real and relevant.

> ## Why video classroom talk?
>
> ➤ To inform reflective practice
> ➤ To see or hear what often goes unnoticed
> ➤ To understand the student perspective about what is being learned and why
> ➤ To pick up on students' misunderstandings
> ➤ To make the habitual practices (of student and teacher) visible.

Video recordings are especially helpful in allowing teachers to revisit what is said, what this reveals about teaching and learning and what happens as a consequence of what is said. It allows us to change what we do and compare and reflect upon what happens when we make these changes. There are, however, less intrusive ways of exploring what happens in our classrooms, the most common being a formal classroom observation.

Classroom observations

Classroom observations can be an easy, time-effective way of answering very simple questions about what happens in our classrooms. A simple example might be to ask yourself how many different opportunities for talk do you create as a teacher, or what is the balance between whole-class talk and group or paired work. Having made this assessment of your own practice it is a simple enough task to keep a log of how much time is spent over a week engaged in these different types of talk. An example of such a log is given in Figure 2.2.

	Interaction					
	Pair	Peer group	Individual	One-to-one with teacher/TA	Group with teacher/TA	Whole-class interactive work
Monday: Lesson 1						
Lesson 2						

Figure 2.2   **Observation schedule recording talk patterns**

A log such as this will not tell you what is a preferable balance in terms of activities but it can reveal patterns of interaction in your own classroom that may surprise you and that you may wish to change. Discovering that the 15 minutes you thought was spent in whole-class interactive sessions was more commonly 25 minutes might prompt a change in what you do with this time. Asking a Teaching Assistant to log teacher talk and child talk in this time might further reveal patterns of interaction that had not been visible before. There is no golden ratio in terms of what this balance might be but discovering that 'interactive' really means you talk and children listen can be salutary.

Observing the patterns of engagement amongst children within whole-class interactive activities can also be revealing. Teachers are well aware of the fact that not all children engage with equal enthusiasm in whole-class teaching episodes. For a teacher working with up to 30 children, following the individual participation of any one child is impossible, particularly if children are quietly disengaging. Using structured observation, however, can be informative for any teacher wishing to track the participation of individual children, or groups of children in their class. An example of an observation schedule is given in Figure 2.3.

Name	Behaviour							
	Asks question	Invited to answer	Initiates talk	Shouts out on task	Shouts out off task	Joins in activity	Talks to peer	Puts hand up	Off task

Figure 2.3   Observation schedule recording participation levels

Clearly this schedule requires an independent observer to be sitting in on the lesson, with no other responsibility other than completing the schedule by tallying in the appropriate boxes when a given behaviour occurs. What systematic observation offers is a picture of how engaged or disengaged selected children are, and how successfully teachers hold the attention of, for example, low-attaining children. Adapting the schedule to record 'off task' behaviour every five minutes, might reveal at what point in the session children become disengaged. If there is a general tendency for low attainment children to be less engaged after 10 to 15 minutes, for example, then this argues strongly for keeping the whole-class sessions shorter, or including more variety in the opportunities to participate. If observing children in different talk contexts reveals that certain children engage more in paired talk than in whole-class talk, then this might influence how you structure different sessions for different purposes. A schedule of this kind is clearly quite revealing in observing the impact of changes in classroom practice on individuals or groups of children.

A common observation of groups of children interacting with a single teacher is that certain children stand out as being more vocal, are more frequently given the floor or are more generally noticeable than others. A schedule such as this would not be needed to identify those children who are keen participants or who are often disruptive or who shout out. What a schedule can reveal, however, is how generally inclusive these sessions are. Clearly there will be children who will dominate question and answer times and others who rarely contribute, but as teachers we are more likely to be aware of those on the extremes than the majority whose participation may not give us cause for concern, but who may be being overlooked. This might argue for having a greater variety of interactive activities that don't rely on individuals volunteering to take part, such as paired talk or recording an answer to a question on a whiteboard then holding it up. Another example of how an observation might impact on practice might be in recording how many times any given child is invited to answer a question. The nature of these whole-class episodes is such that a child's opportunity to contribute is almost entirely governed by whether the teacher selects them to speak or not. In a class of 30 children, and a time period of less than 20 minutes, no one child will be given many opportunities to speak, a pertinent question might be how many children never speak at all? Various strategies have been developed in the light of this finding, such as experimenting with 'no hands up' policies, or replacing question and answer times with more inclusive formats. The column recording how many questions children ask can be revealing, as previous research has suggested that the answer to this is 'not many'. Consciously preparing a whole-class activity which encourages children to ask the questions can be an obvious consequence of responding to what is discovered through a formal observation.

Systematically observing children who seem to be reluctant participants might be revealing, but care has to be taken in interpreting what is observed: a child who sits quietly and rarely volunteers information, might still be highly engaged, while a child with their hand permanently in the air might be doing so habitually rather than because they have anything to say. Nevertheless, taken together the behaviours that imply engagement and those that imply disengagement, together with the opportunity to track certain children and get a picture of what kinds of talk activities will increase or decrease their levels of engagement, can be informative and can impact on practice. Explicit observation of this kind can provide the third eye that teachers themselves can never have when they are involved with directing talk to facilitate the learning of up to 30 children.

Analysing examples of children's writing

The research project that informs this book is concerned with the interface between talking and writing. The use of video and classroom observations allows an insight into different talk activities, both the impact of teacher-led interactive sessions and teacher-designed child-to-child talk opportunities. What is more difficult to unpick, however, is how, indeed if, these talk opportunities support writing. Chapter 5 provides a detailed outline of how a small sample of children's writing can be viewed in terms of the lesson that generated it, and in particular in terms of the link between classroom talk and written text. The Talk to Text Project invested a lot of time in analysing both the talk and the text generated from individual lessons, time that is not a luxury available to busy classroom teachers, nevertheless it is possible that reflecting on children's writing can inform classroom pedagogy.

Teachers' assessments of children's writing are generally undertaken to monitor individual progress, and to assess how well individual children have understood the learning objectives of a given lesson. Taken as a whole, however, the writing produced from any lesson can be considered in terms of what it might reveal about the success or otherwise of certain activities or more generally of particular pedagogical approaches. Seeing children's writing as an artefact of the lesson that produced it rather than the child that produced it, requires teachers to think about the relationship between how writing tasks are set up and how this impacts upon the writing produced.

Questions you might ask of a set of writing samples from the same lesson might be:

- How similar or different are they – does this matter?

- Which ideas are most commonly written down – where did these ideas come from?

- Which ideas are quirkily original – where did these ideas come from?

- Are the talk activities discernible in the texts – how?

- Which talk activities have most impact on the text?

- How does the writing compare to your own expectations?

- Are you disappointed or pleased with the writing – why?

Having an observation of the participation levels of certain children can make visible individual differences – there may be children who write very much more than they say while others say very much more than they are able to write, and so the talk activities may be supporting these children in very different ways.

> How (if at all) might an increase in talk activities support the child who says very little?
>
> How (if at all) might an increase in talk activities support the child who writes very little?
>
> How might talking and listening be supporting writing?
>
> How might teachers encourage active listening?

A further possibility is to use examples from the children's writing to generate future talk activities. These might include:

- Representing as many different versions of the same idea as possible to discuss the huge variety of possible ways of saying the same thing – this might encourage thinking about reshaping a sentence in a different way

- Discussing different opening/closing sentences

- Highlighting the most common sentence or idea and trying to find as many different ways of saying it

- Bringing unusual or original ideas from their writing and discussing what makes them original:

  o   The idea itself
  o   The way the idea is written down.

Interviewing the children

In the Talk to Text project children from both the project and comparison schools were interviewed at the beginning and end of the project in order to understand their attitudes to writing itself: whether it was viewed as easy or difficult, whether it was enjoyed or not or when it was enjoyed or not. The children were also asked what made 'good' writing or 'good' writers. The findings from these interviews are discussed in Chapter 7, here we suggest ways in which interviewing children might prove a helpful way of both informing practice and supporting learning.

An interview is another talk opportunity; a means of giving children the floor. If talking through ideas does provide an opportunity to make and construct meaning, then what is generally viewed as a research tool can hold possibilities for facilitating learning. Talking to children about their writing has been a focus of several research projects undertaken by the team. Encouraging children to think about what they have written, why they have crossed out certain words or sentences or why they made changes were questions asked for the purposes of research, but in attempting to articulate their understanding children have often been enabled to render implicit knowledge, both about the content and the process of writing, explicit. The following interview schedule might help children to evaluate their own work. It could be a Teaching Assistant that asks the questions, but getting the children to interview each other might change the dynamic of the conversation, as the interviewer would not be seen as sitting in judgement on the writing. If you do this it might be a good idea to make a recording of it for you to listen to later.

What is your writing about?

Which idea (sentence/word) do you think is the best? – Why?

Is there anything you might change? – How?

For writing lessons that have a very clear learning objective, such as using formal language, or writing instructions, or using connectives, interviewing children about what they have understood or what they thought the purpose of the lesson was can be revealing. A possible interview schedule might be:

What do you think was the most important thing you have learned in this lesson?

Did you know anything about this already? Tell me what you knew.

Did you find anything hard to understand?

If you had to explain this to your mum and dad, how would you explain it? Pretend you're the teacher!

It could be a salutary experience to discover what children believe your carefully planned lesson, complete with clearly defined aims and objectives, was actually about. While a researcher might use an interview of this type to check what the children had taken away from the lesson, from a teaching and learning perspective an interview such as this makes visible any discrepancy between what the teacher believes they have taught and what the child reveals they have learned.

In an Action Research context it is possibly in the conducting of interviews where it is revealed what it is that makes a teacher, a teacher, and a researcher, a researcher. When teachers conduct interviews with children they find it almost impossible not to be in the role of a teacher for those children. Supporting the children in their thinking, leading them towards answers, framing their understanding, all came so naturally. Researchers, however, are far more ruthless: taking a child's answer at face value, demanding that they explain what they mean and asking unhelpful questions such as 'Can you say more about that?' are common talk patterns. In spite of this ruthlessness, those of us who research with children find that the vast majority of children love being interviewed, they like having a place where what they say is the focus, not what they should have said. The questions are not like classroom questions, there genuinely are no wrong answers. Researchers do not know the answers to the questions they ask because they do not know the child providing the answers, nor what they think or how they think. What matters for the researcher is how children's answers differ, and what those differences reveal, not how well the answers conform to a learning objective. The one-to-one attention, together with the impression that the focus is on what the child thinks, makes interviewing free of the need to teach or foster learning, and in this sense it is completely neutral. The researcher is not trying to communicate anything to the child, rather she is trying to make it possible for the child to communicate with the researcher. This being so, for a teacher to interview children from their own class might prove difficult both for the teacher and the child, when the roles of teacher and learner are so clearly established. The possibility of using children to interview each other has already been suggested; other alternatives might include teachers interviewing children from other classes. Using Teaching Assistants, Meal Time Assistants or parents might be other possibilities.

> How many opportunities do children have to 'think aloud' – without feeling that their thoughts are being assessed? How could you find this out?

Conclusions

A common discourse around the role of the teacher in the current educational climate is the argument that teaching is undervalued and that teachers are becoming deskilled by being positioned as the deliverers of a curriculum largely designed by others and taught through strategies developed and disseminated via a top-down model. Thus it has been reduced to the Cinderella profession. At the same time, however, there is a movement amongst the teaching profession to engage in reflective practice, to claim the role of the 'expert' in their own classrooms and to develop a bottom-up approach to strategic initiatives which resists the one-size-fits-all approach to teaching. Action research is just one of the ways in which this is expressed and the methods described here are just some of the ways in which teachers can look for evidence to inform these initiatives.

Interlude 1

Being Involved in Research – the View From a School

Frances Dunkin

Head teacher at Field Place First School during the Talk to Text project

At Field Place we worked with the School of Education at Exeter University on two research projects: 'The Talk Project' between 1999 and 2003 and 'Talk to Text', 2003–2004. Having been appointed to the post of head teacher in 1997, the engagement with the university was crucial in developing and realising my vision for Field Place.

The impact of the work can be seen in the following quote from our OFSTED report in 2007 in which the leadership and management of the school was graded 1:

> [the headteacher has a] sharp awareness of how to raise standards. Self-evaluation systems are outstanding and informed accurately by detailed analyses of pupils' standards and progress. Recent improvements in the teaching and learning of reading, for example, were the result of prompt action to rectify weaknesses in pupils' skills in reading unfamiliar words.

Working with Exeter University as a partner

> The school has developed very good partnerships with other schools and universities that provide valuable expertise as well as useful sharing of ideas and facilities. (OFSTED, 2007)

In developing the quality of teaching for learning at Field Place the engagement with colleagues at the School of Education was invaluable in explaining, providing coaching for, and modelling the research process for myself and colleague head teachers. The structuring of a research project, the use of data and the questioning of how children learned, for example in the introduction of the National Strategies, gave the school the opportunity to engage actively in this as a learning process and not just passively to accept received wisdom.

The value placed by these research projects on the quality of teaching and learning emphasised the primary focus that this was for the school, and the time that staff gained for research through external funding was crucial to their success. The opportunity to engage in this way ensured that those areas identified as needing development through the self-review process had the opportunity for support from the research community (e.g. children's writing through the Talk to Text project).

The impact on teaching for learning

Engaging with the university radically changed our understanding of the learning/teaching process. Although the numbers of staff and children directly involved were a minority, the projects were shared with all staff as part of the school development process and were implemented across the school. In working with both university and school colleagues we saw the impact of working together on teaching and learning and that through this we developed new knowledge: the co-construction of knowledge. This shaped our understanding of how children learned and became the basis of the development of our teaching for learning policy.

The 'strap line' for the school became: 'Love to learn together'.

The impact on children's learning

In our research projects the value that was placed on children as learners rather than on teachers' teaching caused a fundamental shift to the focus of the school: children were recognised and valued as partners in their learning, with acknowledgement of their own prior experiences and enquiring and creative minds. In making judgements as to what makes a 'good' lesson the engagement of children and their contribution to the learning were seen as key. Interviews with children after the lesson provided valuable insights into what worked for them. In monitoring children's progress, the research approach, the use of a wide range of data both 'hard' and 'soft' as evidence, became embedded in the school's development and review process. This was recognised by OFSTED in their comments on self-review.

Personalising learning

Alongside the research projects the school developed its own tracking and target-setting system which supported the research through teachers' and the senior leadership team's ability to monitor children's learning and progress. The impact of the research projects and a range of interventions that were introduced to ensure that all children, including those with special educational needs, made good progress were monitored through the use of this tracking system. 'Family Learning', and early literacy interventions were monitored for their impact on children's progress and the review built into the development, or not, of the programmes. This was developed as part of the National Foundation for Educational Research (NFER) 'Researching the Research-Engaged School' research project.

The impact on school staff: developing a learning community

The opportunity for teachers to engage in research with university colleagues cannot be overestimated in terms of their understanding of learning as the prime focus for them as professionals and the value it gave to what they did in the classroom every day. Engaging in research provided professional development activities for the staff involved, but, again through the focus on school development, gave all staff the opportunity to learn. Thus when engaged in the Talk to Text project, children's writing was a key area for development for the school and a 'Talk to Text' conference with presentations by university colleagues and teachers from other schools in addition to those based at Field Place meant that all teachers and support assistants learned and wanted to use the research findings to develop their own teaching for learning. This then became embedded and built into the English policy from which new staff could learn.

Most teachers who had engaged in the research projects went on to further research, including an MA in education – and later a headship. As head teacher I was able to coach in the research process and model ways of working and this was evident when the school was asked to be part of the NFER Project 'Researching the Research-Engaged School'. This gave the opportunity to two young members of staff to develop research skills working with colleagues and researchers from other contexts and to present their own research into the impact of school-based interventions on children's learning.

The use of research tools, especially the use of video, provided another real step for staff development. In addition to the focused classroom observations by the senior leadership team, *all* teachers were videoed teaching, which they used for their own self-reflection. In reviews of professional development this was identified as being of great value, a real learning experience. The next step is to use video for coaching and modelling outstanding lessons.

The school and the wider learning community

The opportunity to work collaboratively with other schools in the locality meant that schools could learn from each other's strengths. We developed strong networks as head teachers and teaching staff, and all learned from each other. Our Talk to Text Conference was noted for the contribution of the newly qualified teacher engaged in research as well as the university colleague. These strong links have provided a force for development in new initiatives across the locality of schools and in looking at new models of leadership.

As a group of head teachers we were asked to disseminate our research at West Sussex Head Teachers Conferences and at presentations for new head teachers, encouraging them to take a research-based approach to school development. Disseminating our research and attending British and European research conferences gave us further insight into learning for teaching and allowed us to enjoy being part of the wider community of teacher researchers engaged in developing our shared understanding of children's learning.

3 Talk to Generate Ideas

Ros Fisher

Introduction

This chapter addresses the first of our strategic elements of talk for writing: idea generation. Using talk to help children collect and extend ideas for writing is not new. Class discussion, brainstorming, role play, etc. have long been activities used as precursors to writing. In the Talk to Text project this was the aspect with which teachers felt most comfortable. They had plenty of ideas about what to do and willingly shared these with the research team and each other.

One thing that emerged clearly from the data was that the organisation of the talk was of great importance. Just having a good idea and getting children to talk a lot did not necessarily result in good writing. In fact, on some occasions, the mere amount of talk and volume of ideas became overwhelming and resulted in very little written work or in an incomplete piece. The idea of talk supporting writing with early writers is to help them deal with the fact that writing requires using a whole lot of skills all at once. Getting ideas to write about is but one aspect of this. Having no ideas is obviously unhelpful but having too many ideas and no notion of how to craft those ideas together is just as unhelpful.

How can you get a balance between helping children with ideas and the risk of taking away their creativity?

Supporting children in developing ideas for the content of their writing helps all children. However, it can be particularly helpful for children for whom English is not their first language. Not only will it help them sort out their ideas but talk with a first-language English speaker can extend the additional language speaker's English vocabulary and help develop understanding of the new culture.

The demands of learning our writing system are even greater for children who find school work difficult. Talk will help them think up and extend their ideas but also, in the Talk to Text project, seemed to help them gain a better understanding of the writing task set by the teacher. Later in this chapter, the example of the children talking about a beach safety poster, gave them the chance to talk about the poster in a general way before clarifying the task set and getting down to writing.

Some of the talk activities that teachers use will be discussed under the following headings:

- Role play

- Drawing on experience

- Using pictures

- Using artefacts

- Telling others.

The second part of the chapter considers how the teacher can scaffold ideas and examines closely one longer extract of children's talk while writing.

We have tried to group the kinds of talk activities together here but, in reality, it is difficult to allocate categories. Stories were used regularly in a variety of different ways. In each of the activities described below, teachers encouraged children to use talk to help them think about what they were going to write. In the most successful of the activities they also used the talk to structure the writing activity in a way that reduced the demand on these young writers rather than increased it.

Role play

Teacher-in-role

The advantage of teacher-in-role is that it lets the teacher keep control of the talk and ensure that it stays within the focus of the topic. When reading *The Rainbow Bear* by Michael Morpurgo, one teacher took the part of the polar bear who had been caught and trapped in a cage. The book is full of colourful language, particularly about the time when the bear roams free on the ice and fishes in the cold waters. Once captured and placed in a cage the bear is, not surprisingly, unhappy.

In order to reinforce the idea of being in-role, the teacher had brought in a toy polar bear that she held while talking. To emphasise the sadness of the bear, she slumped in her chair and changed the tone of her voice. The children had to ask the bear questions about why he was so unhappy. The 'bear' explained about being bored, not liking the food, being scared by all the people looking at him and so on.

The episode of teacher-in-role was not an isolated activity but a part of the sort of build up to a piece of writing that this teacher used regularly. This was the second day that the class had worked on the story of the rainbow bear. The previous lesson had focused on the joyful times the bear enjoyed while free. The lesson on the second day, described here, started with a picture from the book shown on the white board. Here the rainbow bear is looking sad in his cage. Children first looked at the picture and worked in talk partners to come up with words that told how the bear was feeling. They suggested words such as: lonely, miserable, grumpy, tearful, etc. The teacher-in-role episode came next when the children used the words they had thought up in pairs to ask the bear why he was feeling lonely, miserable, grumpy, tearful, etc. The teacher provided reasons based on the difference between his lifestyle before and after capture: 'I'm so miserable because I can't swim in the sea'; 'I'm lonely because I have no other bears to play with'.

Following the role play, the teacher reviewed with children why the bear was sad. The lesson then moved to the oral rehearsal stage as children again worked in talk partners to come up with sentences about the bear.

> I am heartbroken because I am locked in a cage with only a little bit of food.
>
> I am terrified because people keep laughing and pointing at me.
>
> I am lonely because there are no seals to catch.

Thus through careful orchestration children had the vocabulary and the ideas to create their own sentences based on the story. Not only did they have the opportunity to give and hear different ideas, but the talk activities themselves led them to use complex sentences with a connective in a natural way. Those children who find writing difficult, have been able to use their knowledge of spoken language to contribute to the lesson.

When the teacher takes a role, he/she is able to feed into the interaction the sort of words and sentences that he/she would like children to use. He/she can place emphasis on particular aspects of a story or other form of writing. He/she can ask questions of the children that allow them to respond as experts, reversing the normal pattern of teacher–child interaction.

One of the pieces of writing that came from this lesson was

> I am upset because there is no room to play in.
>
> I am miserable because I miss the lovely smell of seal.
>
> I am terrified because of all the people staring at me.

Getting into role

It is always surprising how children accept so readily that their teacher has suddenly become someone different. They seem perfectly able to make the switch. All that is needed is some signal to indicate what is happening. In the case described above the teacher introduced the toy bear, told the class that he wanted to talk to them, changed her voice and demeanour and the class accepted her new role without question. Other ploys that can work well are putting on a hat or cloak or leaving the room and coming back in as the character. As with other things, the more familiar the activity, the easier it is to make the switch. Puppets can be a good way in to using role play as a teacher.

Children-in-role

Introducing simple forms of role play for children to take part in also provides them with the chance to explore ideas before writing. This can be particularly helpful for children for whom English is an additional language as they get the chance to hear other ways of saying things and can practise the ideas for themselves.

One example of a simple form of role play was seen during work centred around the story of *Billywise* by Judith Nicholls. The writing was to be about the moment in the story when Billywise, the young owl, is trying to pluck up the courage to fly. The writing task was for children to write speech bubbles for what Billywise's mother is saying to the baby owl to help him pluck up the courage to fly and for Billywise's reply. Here the teacher used a strategy sometimes called Conscience Alley. The children got into their talk pairs and then stood opposite each other holding hands in the air high enough for other children to walk under. This created a corridor of arms that children could walk through. Children on one side of the corridor were designated as the mother and on the other side as the frightened baby owl. Two children at a time walked through the corridor and as they walked the children on one side were encouraging them to be brave, to fly, while children on the other side were reminding them how scary it was, how far up and how dangerous. Each child got a chance to walk through the corridor and all children got a chance to be both the mother owl and the baby owl. Both through saying and listening they all got a wealth of ideas to take to their own writing.

Conscience Alley could also be used with the story of *Little Red Riding Hood* with one side as her mother warning her about the danger in the wood and the other side being the wolf tempting her in. Most stories provide some sort of situation where a choice has to be made.

In the first of the two lessons on *The Rainbow Bear* the teacher re-read a page which describes how the bear enjoyed playing in the water or on the ice. She asked children first of all to talk in pairs to suggest some words that told what the bear was doing. They came up with ideas such as tumbling, sliding, plunging, diving, and so on. Then children moved to stand in a circle and made a statue of one of the words they had talked about. When they had all made a statue, certain children showed theirs and the others had to guess the word that went with the statue. Again this sort of activity is useful to support children for whom English is an additional language as the words are reinforced by action.

Writing-in-role

As well as talking-in-role as a preparation for writing, writing-in-role is also a useful activity. However, it is not easy for young children and is something that needs building up gradually through talk both in and out of role. When working on the story of *The Kiss that Missed* by David Melling, the teacher got children to write a letter in-role. In the story, the little prince gets very fed up because his father, the king, never kisses him goodnight properly. He just rushes past the bedroom door and blows a kiss through the doorway: every night the kiss misses. This kind of experience is one that is familiar to young children. It was not hard for them to talk to their partners and share how they would feel in this situation. With a class of beginning writers, it was clear that the letter would not be long. The teacher identified two things that would be included in the body of the letter: what the child was feeling and what they wanted their father to do about it. This gave the opportunity for two episodes of paired talk. In the first, children shared ideas about how they were feeling. In-role as the prince they told their partner (their father) what they felt at night when all he did was blow a goodnight kiss to them and it missed. In the second occasion of paired talk, they took turns in the role as prince to tell their father what they wanted him to do instead of just blowing a kiss. Here the paired talk plays the part of both idea generation and oral rehearsal. Through talk they can try out a variety of ideas about how they are feeling as well as trying out different ways of expressing those feelings. The actual writing of the letter in-role became a far simpler task than it would have been had they not been able to try out the ideas beforehand. For those at the very early stages of writing or who find writing difficult often talk is just enough without needing to proceed to writing.

Other role-play techniques that could be used to help children develop ideas for the content of their writing are set out below.

Freeze-frames

These are tableaux where it is literally as though the film has been frozen. They are used to explore a specific incident or event. Individual children or groups have to create a still (i.e. unmoving) scene to represent characters at a significant moment in a story. They can be used on their own or as a sequence to build up a story. The talk that goes into making the tableau gives children a chance to try out and develop ideas. A simple version of this was described earlier when children were asked to make a statue of the rainbow bear. See the lessons at the end of this chapter for a sample lesson using freeze-frame.

Thought tracking

This can develop from a freeze-frame. Focusing on one of the characters in the tableau the rest of the class can stand or sit around the frame and say aloud the thoughts of a particular character. This is a good technique for exploring the thoughts of characters before writing part of a story or a piece of dialogue.

Mime

Although the topic here is talk, mime is also a useful way of getting children to try out ideas. It can be particularly helpful for children whose spoken language is not fluent. It gives children time to think about their roles and the kinds of language they might use. This could move on to spoken role play and then writing.

Hot-seating

Hot-seating involves the class in asking questions of someone in-role as a character, who sits on the 'hot-seat'. This character can either be the teacher, as in the example above, or a child. The questions can be prepared or improvised. It is important here that all children are familiar with the character either from a story or real life. It is also a good way of exploring the gaps in a narrative and helping young writers move beyond simple retelling.

Forum theatre (adapted)

A small group of children act out a scene while the rest of the class watch them. The class comment on the scene and make suggestions as to how they might behave or speak in a different way. It is a useful strategy for considering alternative ideas for a narrative. See the lessons at the end of this chapter for a sample lesson using this technique.

Telephone conversations

This involves pairs of children improvising a telephone dialogue between two characters at a difficult moment in the story. A variation could include the teacher speaking as one character while the rest of the class take turns to speak as the other character.

Paired improvisation

Pairs are given roles or agree them for themselves relevant to the writing that they are going to do. They begin a dialogue on a signal, making the conversation up as they go along. The teacher then signals when to stop. This can be done with two or three different pairings giving alternative versions to stimulate ideas.

Experience

Giving children the opportunity to write from their own experience ensures that they do have something to write about. The experience must be something that you can be sure they do have experience of – as in the example when the writing is about their own immediate environment. Alternatively, the experience can be one that is provided for them during school time.

One example of the teacher providing the experience for the class was during work also centred around the story of *Billywise* by Judith Nicholls. This was in a different classroom from the one described above. The writing was to be about the same moment in the story when Billywise, the young owl, is trying to pluck up the courage to fly. The writing task was for the children to write what Billywise's mother is saying to the baby owl to help him pluck up the courage to fly. Before starting writing the teacher built up their interest and experience to help support them when it came to writing. First of all she took all the class out onto the playground to a tree house they had in an activity area. The children had the chance to stand in the tree house and imagine what it would be like to have to jump out and fly. (Note: of course, the teacher took all sensible precautions to make sure that this was conducted safely and that the children understood that they should not actually try to fly!)

When they went back to the classroom they were able to draw on the experience of standing high up looking down and imagining what it would be like to have to fly. The children were encouraged to think of different words for how they felt. The sort of words that the children came up with were: anxious, terrified, frightened, petrified. This raises the interesting question as to how much the experience has to feed directly into the words and ideas used for writing. It is to be assumed that the teacher did not put her class into a situation in which they really felt terrified and petrified.

The paired talk that followed was the richer for this experience. What is more, the paired talk was supported by an addition of role play with puppets. As part of their work on the story of Billywise, children had made simple paper puppets of owls. Using these the children worked in pairs, taking turns at being the owl baby, Billywise, or the owl mother. In each case they rehearsed the words that mother and baby would say.

In this case the talk relating to idea generation blended easily into the next stage of the writing process: oral rehearsal (see Chapter 4). The children gained ideas for the content of the writing and were then helped to frame how these ideas would be expressed.

Another example of drawing on children's experience was in the writing of a simple poem about the part of town in which the children lived. The lesson started with the children all together on the carpet watching a slide show of pictures from the area around the school. These showed a church, the train station, a thatched pub, the park, and so on. As they looked at the pictures, the teacher encouraged the children to say something about each location. Without using the word 'adjective', what was highlighted were various adjectives that went with each item: the ancient cottage, the noisy school, the peaceful church.

To support the transfer of the children's ideas about the location into writing, the teacher asked the children to draw a rudimentary map. They had to choose six to eight places to visit on their walk around the neighbourhood. In pairs, they drew a few of the features from the area that they had been talking about. The map was no more than an approximate circular route – no attempt was made to consider geographical accuracy. They used arrows drawn on the map to indicate the route they would take.

Only after the two talk activities were complete did the lesson involve writing. The teacher provided the children with a list of prepositions for them to use to describe their walk: over, along, beside, under, and so on. Each pair were given a number of strips of white paper. Each strip was used for one phrase: beside the ancient cottage; under the noisy railway line, and so on.

The final stage of this carefully orchestrated lesson was for the pair to look at the six to eight phrases they had written and decide which order would be best for their poem. Having the phrases written on separate pieces of paper made discussion of the order in which they should come easier. The children could physically move each piece and try out different orders. When they had decided on the order they had to stick each phrase on a larger sheet of paper to produce their poem.

It is easy to criticise such a carefully scripted activity as taking away a lot of opportunity for children to express their own ideas. However, it can also be argued that by giving the children a limited choice, the teacher enabled them to make some genuine if limited compositional choices without overloading them with too much to think about as they wrote. Chapter 1 explores in greater depth how cognitive overload makes the task of writing more difficult for beginning writers. This is particularly the case for those who are struggling and those who have the added challenge of writing in a language that is not familiar to them.

Using pictures

Pictures are another accessible way to provide a stimulus for talking and writing. The following dialogue took place when pairs of children had been given an A3 poster of hazards at the beach. They were asked to talk about what was danger-ous and to think about what they would put on an information sheet about staying safe at the beach. The poster shows many different groups of people doing more or less dangerous things on a beach. It shows hazardous activities such as children playing football on the edge of a cliff and there is an overloaded boat.

In the dialogue below, two children who had been judged by their teacher to be underachieving in writing are just beginning to talk about the poster. The two children start by looking at the picture and talking about the danger. Notice how their tendency at the beginning is to make a story about the picture rather than think about what would be written on an information sheet.

1	*Crystal*	He's the one who needs help.
2	*Jamie*	Look at that …
3	*Crystal*	He's the one that needs help because there's probably a thunder storm …
4	*Jamie*	[Points] look at the football. Look at him, if it [the ball] goes in and he dives he is going to jump into the water.
5	*Crystal*	If that goes into the water I don't think he will jump in.
6	*Jamie*	No but he does it by accident.
7	*Crystal*	He would just walk round the cliffs and …
8	*Teacher*	Remember please you have got the big picture to look at. You decide what information you are going to put on your information sheet. It's about staying safe at the beach.

9	Jamie	Don't play football on the cliffs.
10	Crystal	Don't jump off that rock.
11	Jamie	Don't go through …
12	Crystal	Don't go swimming past … in … near the red flags [Both pause] Don't have too many people in the boat.
13	Jamie	Don't go right out to there.
14	Jamie	Some people should – half should come off … so they wait on the rocks so the other people go on there.
15	Crystal	I think he isn't going to jump. He is just doing fishing.
16	Jamie	No, I was talking about the boat. Oh no he isn't going to jump he is just doing fishing.
17	Crystal	Slip slap slop on …
18	Jamie	Slip on a T-shirt, slop on some sun cream and
19	Crystal	Slip on a sun hat.

Here the picture gives them a chance to explore some ideas together about the picture. Other children on the table are saying similar things and some ideas move from pair to pair. The high attaining pair of writers on the same table begins in a very organised way by discussing how to lay out their information sheet and what their headline should be. Thus the opportunity to talk before starting on the writing allows the pairs of children to consider the topic in their own way before becoming more focused in response to the teacher's instructions.

The two children featured in the dialogue, although behind the others in their ability to produce written script, show that they have understood the task, have some good ideas and know the appropriate ways to express them (9–12). They also have a feel for the language with the 'slip on a T-shirt, slop on some sun cream …' (17–19). If the final written product is incomplete or shows poor secretarial skills, they have at least had good experience of composition. Music can also be used to help children develop ideas as in the sample lesson on pages 62–63.

Using artefacts

As well as pictures, a whole range of artefacts can be used to help stimulate talk to generate ideas for writing. Whether it is a collection of artefacts from a museum linked to a history project or a selection of objects from a rubbish bin, things can generate all kinds of discussion prior to writing. Consider what sort of writing might come from the following artefacts:

- A box with a key, a dead flower and a piece of silk

- A treasure map

- An empty sandwich box, a crushed crisp packet and an empty smoothie bottle

- A suitcase with a pair of shorts, a sweatshirt and one shoe

- An old bottle with a scrunched up (inaccessible) piece of paper inside

- And so on …

Telling others

In any writing that adults do there is an audience (even if it is only for themselves) and a purpose. Most writing done in classrooms is for the teacher, embodying both purpose and audience. Although it is not realistic always to come up with a genuine purpose and audience, it is possible. For example, most authors have websites where it is possible to contact them, or letters can be written to parents, other schools, pen pals, etc. A book to introduce new children to the school or class is a useful group project with a genuine purpose and audience.

One activity that teachers on the Talk to Text project tried was getting children to write for another class to help them with their writing. One such activity was when a Year 2 class wrote to a younger class to advise them on how to write instructions. The video-tape of this lesson shows the two children who were underachieving in writing. In fact, the actual task was challenging for them. Having to provide instructions for someone else to write instructions was confusing but, through careful scaffolding by the teacher, they did have a useful discussion and came up with good advice.

The lesson started with the teacher reminding them about the instructions that they had written the day before. The first talk activity was to talk to their partner about what they remembered about writing instructions. The teacher then explained that the younger class was going to be writing instructions the next day and their teacher wanted this class to help. The next paired talk activity was for each pair to come up with some instructions. They were given several strips of paper and had to write one instruction on each strip.

The two children who were the focus for the video started by putting points about writing in general. These were points that they had heard many times such as 'Don't forget your capital letters' and 'Don't put full stops in the middle of your sentence'. After some input from the teacher, they did move on to think about instructions that were more appropriate to the type of writing such as 'Don't say please' and 'Use bossy words'. What is interesting about these ideas is that both children have clearly taken the teacher's advice and put it into their own words. These instructions are not ones that they have copied off a list of ideas on the white board but their own interpretation of what is needed. Here the talk has not only given them ideas of what to write but has reinforced lessons about writing.

In this lesson, the teacher was quite willing to accept all ideas from the children. The higher attaining writers did come up with useful instructions for the writing of a set of instructions. On the other hand, those who found writing more difficult were encouraged to put whatever seemed important to them in their writing. It was only towards the end of the lesson that the teacher drew attention to which were the most important for writing instructions and then got children to choose the most important. These were written on the white board and printed off to give to the other class.

> How often do you give children the opportunity to write for someone other than the teacher?
> What do you do to help children with ideas for writing that is not described here?

Talk while writing

Most of the ideas given above involve talking together before going to write. One quote from a teacher from the early days of the project sums up some of the difficulties of linking talk directly to the writing:

> I try to do a lot of discussion about everything, um, just to sort of get their ideas, to then build on their ideas from the foundations really. I think talking stops when they then have to go off and perhaps produce a written piece of work. ... It's when, especially in literacy, when you say 'right, I'd like you to go and write an ending to [the] story' [the one] that we've just talked about, that we've all just written together, we've all been really tuned into this for the last fifteen minutes, but when they come to go off to write the ending, it's 'they lived happily ever after' ... once they go away to that table that's it, that's them with a blank piece of paper and a pencil, um, what, what do they do? And, and I think that's when the talking stops.

Not all the children in the project found it easy to work collaboratively on their writing. Often it would be a case of taking turns but without very much talk going on before each turn. The example given below, however, shows how it can work.

In the following transcript the two children have been asked to write a story about finding something on a beach. As a whole-class introduction the teacher had produced a collection of things that they could introduce into their story. These included a jar of sand, some shells, a bucket and spade, etc. The children had sat in a circle and taken turns to say a sentence about one of the items. They had been encouraged to make their sentences more interesting by using words to describe the item. The transcript starts just after the pair had started writing. You will note how the girl writes more quickly than the boy and sometimes has to wait for him. He sounds out the words aloud as he writes. In the first recorded utterance he is sounding out the spelling of the word 'extremely'.

1	Jamie	Ex tree muh [sounds words as writes]
2	Crystal	I've written 'extremely hot'.
3	Jamie	[Writes] 'extremely hot'. Hot [Says as writes] 'I can feel the …'.
4	Crystal	Sand. What could it be? Silver sand? That pencil's rubbish. [Changes it for another.] That's better.
5	Jamie	Sand. I can feel the sand on my feet. Feet, yes?
6	Crystal	I've done four lines.
7	Jamie	1 2 3 4 5
8	Teacher	[Reads] I can feel the sand on my feet. What does it feel like?
9	Crystal	Squishy [Says and writes] 'It feels squishy'
10	Jamie	Feels
11	Crystal	I've done it – squishy. Right I'll read it out. 'One day I went to the beach. It was extremely hot. I can feel the sand on my feet. It feels squishy'.
12	Jamie	Squishy
13	Crystal	What else?
14	Jamie	Full stop?
15	Crystal	I've done that.
16		[Jamie writes and Crystal watches him.]
17	Crystal	What are you writing?
18	Jamie	Squishy and. I crossed out the full stop and put 'and'. Tickly
19	Crystal	[Writes] 'tickly'
20	Jamie	tickly
21	Crystal	And and and and very and and
22	Jamie	And tickly – full stop? Full stop.

23	*Crystal*	If you do a big full stop like that (draws on table with finger) it'll last for ever.
24	*Jamie*	I saw
25	*Crystal*	a
26	*Jamie*	Little luh ih tuh tuh eh I saw
27	*Crystal*	Crab, was it a crab?
28	*Jamie*	Little Red Riding Hood. She … She had a shiny cloak – yeah? Cuh luh oh kuh – cloak Now what?
29	*Crystal*	It was slippery?
30	*Jamie*	yeah
31		[Jamie and Crystal write]
32	*Crystal*	It was slippery – your go
33	*Jamie*	And …
34	*Crystal*	And what?
35	*Jamie*	There. How do you write 'there'?
36	*Crystal*	Tuh huh eh ruh Tuh huh eh ruh eh
37	*Teacher*	Oh I like the slippery.
38	*Crystal*	I thought of that.
39	*Jamie*	There were shiny
40	*Crystal*	Shiny shoes?
41	*Jamie*	blue
42	*Crystal*	Blue what?
43	*Jamie*	waves
44	*Crystal*	Shiny blue waves – my go.
45	*Jamie*	Waves – full stop. There. How many have I done? 1 2 3 4 5 6 7 8 9 10 11 1 2 3 4 5 6 7 8 9 10 11
46	*Crystal*	I've done 1 2 3 4 5 6 7 8 9 10

47	Jamie	Come on then
48	Crystal	[thinks]
49	Jamie	There was a little baby crab
50	Crystal	orange crab
51	Jamie	There
52	Crystal	Tuh huh eh ruh eh wuh ah There was a little orange crab
53	Jamie	Luh ih tuh tuh eh
54	Crystal	I've done it.
55	Jamie	Little oh ruh
56	Crystal	I've done 11 now. [Taps pencil]
57	Jamie	Orange
58	Crystal	I've done it already.
59	Jamie	Cuh ruh ah buh – there!
60	Crystal	Your go. [Rolls pencil] – It's a rolling pin. There was some sellotape on the beach
61	Jamie	No!
62	Crystal	Yeah – sticky.
63	Jamie	Suddenly a little turtle [says slowly as writes]
64	Crystal	Suddenly a little turtle came out of the water. What have you written? Suddenly – what have you written?
65	Jamie	A little turtle … came
66	Crystal	Cuh ay muh …. [writes] Water Done it!
67	Jamie	[Writes] Water – full stop.
68	Crystal	My go then. [Thinks]
69	Jamie	The turtle was shiny and beautiful?
70	Crystal	Yeah.
71		[Jamie and Crystal write, sounding out some words]

72	*Crystal*	Shiny and beautiful. [Stops and rearranges hair then looks around room.] You thought of my go so I get another go.
73	*Jamie*	Hang on.
74	*Crystal*	I smell the salty sea.
75	*Teacher*	Right. I'm afraid it is time to finish and come and sit on the carpet.
76	*Crystal*	[Whispers] I can smell the salty sea.
77	*Teacher*	In 10, 9 …
78	*Crystal*	Smell the salty sea. [Finishes writing and reminds Jamie] I can smell the salty sea. I can smell the salty sea.

Three different strands of talk run through this piece: the composition; the secretarial aspects; and the monitoring of how much they have written. In addition, Crystal sometimes strays off task when she is looking around or playing with her pencil. It is important to recognise that these instances are generally while she is waiting for Jamie to catch up.

Co-construction of the writing

There are several instances where these two children do work together to build their story. In utterance 3 Jamie says 'I can feel the …' and Crystal finishes his sentence with 'Sand' (4). The same thing happens in utterances 24–25 and 63–64. There are also moments when they show that they are collaborating by checking with the other that they agree with their idea. In utterance 5, he says 'I can feel the sand on my feet. Feet, yes?' Later when Jamie suggests that there is a 'baby crab', Crystal changes it to 'orange crab' (49–50). There is no discussion about the relative quality of either suggestion but they show that they are aware of the choices that can be made by writers and can have an opinion. On the other hand, there is the strange introduction of Little Red Riding Hood (28). There is no evidence elsewhere in the video recording of why this character would make an appearance. In fact on the video it is hard to tell whether just prior to this Jamie is sounding out the spelling of 'little' or is about to write 'turtle' (26). Later (63) he does introduce a turtle into the story and it is possible that he was going to introduce this earlier but was deflected by Crystal suggesting 'crab'. We also get some insight into how they compose in utterance 21. Here Jamie has just added 'tickly' to 'squishy'. They have written, 'I can feel the sand on my feet. It feels squishy and tickly'. Crystal then repeats the word 'and' as though trying to conjure up the next word. She tried 'and very' but does not come up with another adjective to add to 'squishy and tickly'.

Both these children demonstrate that they have knowledge of the secretarial aspects of writing. Their teacher is very insistent on the use of full stops and Jamie, in this transcript, often ends his writing of a sentence by writing and proclaiming 'full stop' (22, 45, 67). He also shows that he has some understanding of the use of full stops by the way he knows to cross out the full stop before adding to his sentence (18). As Jamie writes he regularly sounds out the words that he is writing whereas Crystal mostly writes silently. On the whole they do not concern themselves about spelling but he does ask her how to spell 'there' (35) and she is able to give him the correct spelling.

They are also concerned with the progress of their writing. Twice they count their lines (7, 45–46) and Crystal sounds relieved to have caught up with Jamie when she says, 'I've done 11 now' (56). Despite the fact that she has written the same words as he has, she is concerned by having fewer lines. Crystal seems to be more concerned to take turns. She reminds him that it is his turn (32), her turn (44, 68) and reminds him that she needs another go as he had given the idea for her last go (72). She is also very determined when the session ends to make sure that he gets her idea into his story. Although the teacher has told them to stop, she repeats her sentence five times to make sure that he does not forget what to write (74–78).

Teacher talk versus child talk

The quality of classroom interaction has been a topic of debate for many years. It is well documented that the predominant pattern of interaction in classrooms is a form of dialogue known as IRF. This stands for initiation, response, feedback. Here the teacher asks a question, a child answers and the teacher gives feedback on the answer. For example:

Teacher   Can anyone think what might happen next?

Child   The giant could stomp on the monster.

Teacher   Yes, well done. Good idea.

Child   The giant might be scared. He might run way.

Teacher   Yes, he might run away

And so on.

Although this is a well established and potentially useful form of dialogue, it does have some disadvantages. The pattern of interaction is like the spokes of a wheel with each response going back to the teacher for judgement. Children learn quickly to give the answers that they think the teacher wants. This can give some children advantage over others; either because they are better at working out what is wanted or they are just more confident at talking in front of the class. Of course, these two are closely related as the more a child's ideas are accepted the more confident they will be to contribute.

Below we give an example of dialogue which follows the typical IRF format. It is an imaginary teaching episode that is based on many similar dialogues and will be immediately recognisable to anyone familiar with classroom discussion. In this example the teacher has written the beginning of a story designed to build up suspense. Teacher and children have read through the passage and the teacher has now asked them to say what words or phrases helped to build up the suspense.

Teacher	Can you tell me what you picked out? Jake.
Jake	'The dog barked'. It's like just a short bit and you don't know what …
Teacher	It's a short sentence. That's a really good way of creating suspense. Well done. Sally.
Sally	There's a … a … sclamation … thingy.
Teacher	An exclamation mark. The girl jumped! Well done. Lucy.
Lucy	'She shivered' Perhaps she's scared.
Teacher	Well done. I'm going to draw a line under that. 'She *shivered*'. I used 'shivered' to make you think she is scared. Sandeep.
Sandeep	Something moved in the bushes.
Teacher	Something moved in the bushes. Why do you think I used 'something' there? William.
William	'Cos it might be a tiger'.
Teacher	You don't know what it might be. Kwame.
Kwame	You don't know what it is.
Teacher	You don't know what it is. Right. It could be anything. But we don't know. You are doing really well.

Here the children draw out some ideas from the writing that the teacher has done. Their answers show that they can recognise the features that the teacher has put in her writing and are beginning to be able to say why this is. It is also clear that it is the teacher who does most of the talking.

The advantage of paired talk is that it allows all children to have a say without having to say it in front of the rest of the class. It also allows children who have ideas that may not fit with the teacher's expectations to air these. Children who do not feel confident in their use of English can speak quietly to a partner and could even speak in their home language to a partner who shared that language. If generation of ideas for writing is the purpose, then the language used is not as important as the ideas.

In paired talk it is helpful to give clear guidance about what you want them to talk about. There is a place for open-ended instruction such as: talk to your partner about how the story ends; read the piece on the white board and talk to your partner about what you like about it. It can also be helpful to give very clear and precise instructions about what they should do, such as: 'Think of some good words to decide how Jamie was feeling and decide on the three best ones'; 'Choose a sentence you do not like from the ones on the whiteboard and talk to your partner about how you could make it better'. In this case the children are given the chance to be the experts. Their opinions are given value.

Who does the most talking in your class — you or the children?
What opportunities do you give children to talk about their writing?

Summary of points for the class teacher

- ➤ Supporting children in getting together their ideas for writing *before* they start to write frees up their 'brain power' to concentrate on getting the words down.
- ➤ Teacher-in-role provides the opportunity to show children the sort of words they might use.
- ➤ Paired role-play activities for children allow them to try out their ideas for writing.
- ➤ Pairing up children for whom English is their first language with someone for whom it is not can help both members of the pair.
- ➤ Using children's shared experience for writing provides a more even playing field for children who come from a range of background experiences.
- ➤ Try to find opportunities for children to write for other audiences than the teacher.
- ➤ Think about how your own use of language can help or hinder children thinking up their own ideas.
- ➤ Remember that words are only good or 'powerful' within the context of how they impact on meaning in that piece of writing.

Suggested further reading

Cordon, R. (2002) *Developing Narrative Writing 7–13*. Available from UKLA (www.ukla.org).

Gouch, K., Grainger, T. and Lambirth, A. (2005) *Creativity in Writing*. London: Taylor and Francis.

Lesson plans for idea generation

Idea Generation Activity – Conscience Alley

Purpose: To develop ideas about different viewpoints in preparation for writing.

Summary: Conscience or decision alley is a way of exploring a character's mind at a moment of crisis or decision making. It allows children to investigate the complexity of the decision a character is facing, and to understand differing points of view.

Resources/preparation:
A well-known story, and an episode from the story where a character has to make a decision.

Activity

- Children consider a character in a story who has to make a decision or who has a dilemma.
- The teacher arranges the children so they are standing in two lines facing each other.
- Children in one line represent the ideas of 'the good conscience' in the other the ideas of 'the bad conscience'.
- Children are given 'thinking time' to develop one idea.
- One child in-role walks down the line to listen to the ideas of both sides.
- The ideas are then used as a basis for writing.

Class-based Example

Helen teaches a class of 26 Year 2 children. Over the past week they have been thinking about the story of the three bears and the role of Goldilocks. Helen explains that this morning they are going to the three bears' house to help Goldilocks to make some decisions.

Helen has three bowls of porridge and explains that Goldilocks is very hungry. She splits the class into two groups and explains that one group is Goldilocks' 'good conscience' and the other group is Goldilocks' 'bad conscience'. Group One has to think of ideas why Goldilocks should eat the porridge, Group Two needs to persuade Goldilocks that she shouldn't eat the porridge.

In pairs the children discuss their ideas. Group One comes up with ideas such as – Goldilocks is hungry, the porridge looks tasty, porridge is good for you, the three bears won't mind. Group Two comes up with ideas such as – stealing is wrong, the three bears will be cross, Goldilocks could go home and have some food, the porridge might be poisonous.

The two groups form an alley for Goldilocks to walk through. Helen chooses a child to be Goldilocks and then asks the rest of the class to try to persuade Goldilocks as she walks down conscience alley.

Helen has prepared sheets with speech bubbles for the children to fill in using their ideas. They use the magic pencil technique to practise writing their idea, before returning to their table for writing time (see page 76).

If this is the first time you have tried this activity …

- Show the children a video of other children using the conscience alley technique (NLS professional development DVD 2).
- Allow children to whisper their ideas to begin with, or say their ideas in pairs.
- Allow children to use the same idea as another child.
- Practise several times so that the conscience alley becomes a performance and the children can all hear each other's ideas.

Idea Generation Activity – Forum Theatre

Purpose: To develop ideas in preparation for writing.

Summary: A drama technique that allows children to see an event from a different point of view, or to change the outcome of an event.

Resources/preparation: A well-known story with a tension point.

Activity

- Choose a tension point in a well-known story.
- Children improvise a short scene around the tension point.
- One group shares their scene with the class.
- The teacher asks the class to become 'spect – actors', this means that they can put up their hand and take the place of a character in the improvisation at any point during the action.
- The scene is re-played several times to give the children the opportunity to explore the issues.
- The forum theatre allows children to develop ideas for their writing.

Class-based example

Sue has been working with her class of Year 2 children on the book *Where the Forest Meets the Sea*. They have thought in detail about the rainforest environment and why rainforest is important. Sue has told the children that there is a plan to build a hotel at the edge of the rainforest. This will mean cutting down 200 trees. Sue uses a 'hot-seating' technique to encourage the children to explore different points of view. The children 'hot seat' a 50-year-old man who has lived in the rainforest all his life and the woman who would like to build a hotel.

In pairs the children have a few minutes to imagine they are the forest dweller and the hotel builder. In-role they begin to discuss the plans to build a hotel. Sue chooses one pair to show their short improvisation to the rest of the class. She then splits the class in half explaining that one half are going to help the forest dweller, the other half will help the hotel builder. They are not just an audience but 'spect-actors'. If anyone in the audience can think of more, or different, ideas they put up their hand, and take over the role of either the forest dweller or the hotel builder. The audience can also ask the actors questions in-role, or make suggestions to them.

The children re-run their short scene with the help of the 'spect-actors'. Once the forum theatre is complete, Sue asks the children to work in pairs and write a short script.

If this is the first time you have tried this activity …

- Begin with an issue that is quite polarised, something about which the children are passionate. You need to choose an area where the children will have plenty of ideas.
- Brainstorm ideas for the different characters before you begin the forum theatre.
- Use plenty of teacher modelling. Encourage any additional adults in the classroom to support you with this!

Idea Generation Activity – Freeze-Frame

Purpose: To develop ideas in preparation for writing.

Summary: Freeze-framing is a strategy that allows children to capture a particular moment in a story. It is useful for generating ideas about characters' thoughts and feelings. It can also help with developing an understanding of story structure.

Resources/preparation: A well-known story and enough space for children to create freeze-frames.

Activity

- The teacher explains that the children are going to be making 'still pictures' or 'freeze-frames' of moments in the story they have been reading.
- The class is split into groups, either pairs, or larger groups. They are given a moment from the story to re-create in a still picture and a minute to discuss their ideas.
- The groups share their freeze-frames.
- The teacher says 'one, two, three, freeze'. The children who are acting hold their freeze-frame for a few seconds. The teacher asks those who are watching to take their imaginary cameras out of their pockets and take a photo.

Class-based example

A Year 1 class has been reading the book *We're Going on a Bear Hunt* by Michael Rosen. They are familiar with the story. They sit in a circle with their teacher and look at the pictures of the children going through the mud, river, forest and snow. As a class they discuss what each of these environments would feel like.

The teacher explains that they are going to make the same journey as the family in the book by making still pictures or freeze-frames. The teacher splits the class into groups of six. The first group gather in the centre of the circle. The teacher explains that they need to use their bodies and their faces to show what it would be like to go through the thick oozy mud. The rest of the class take out their imaginary cameras. The teacher says 'one, two, three, freeze' and the group in the centre of the circle hold their freeze-frame for a few seconds. The teacher gives feedback, focusing on children who are using appropriate facial expressions and are remaining in character. The teacher then asks the children in the 'freeze-frame' how it felt to be walking through the mud.

The teacher repeats this sequence for the river, forest and snow. The class gather in the circle again and the teacher explains that each group will be writing about one part of the journey.

If this is the first time you have tried this activity …

- Before you begin the activity make sure the children know how to freeze. You could play musical statues, or grandmother's footsteps.
- Choose a freeze-frame where children can work independently. As children become more confident you can give them time to prepare more complex freeze-frames, at first in pairs, and later in larger groups.

Support the children by saying:

'I really believe you are in the mud/river.'
'Fantastic facial expression.'
'You look really scared/cold/unhappy.'
'Really imagine you are there!'
'Let's look for people who are holding their freeze frames really well.'

Thought tracking

While the children are holding their frozen picture. Tap individuals on the shoulder and ask them to say a word or sentence to explain what they are thinking or how they are feeling.

Idea Generation Activity – Using Music

Purpose: To develop ideas in preparation for writing.

Summary: A piece of music is used to help children use their imagination and develop ideas about a setting.

Resources/preparation: An appropriate piece of music.

Activity

- Ask the children to close their eyes.
- Take them on an imaginary journey to a new place (you can see the school building below you and you fly south, over hills and valleys, over the sea . . .).
- Explain that they have arrived in a new place.
- Use a piece of music to help them visualise this new setting.
- Each child goes on their own imaginary journey.
- Children share their journeys with their writing partner.
- Their ideas can then form the basis for a piece of writing.

Class-based example

Sue works with a group of 26 children who are in Year 2. They have been working with the book *Where the Forest Meets the Sea* and thinking about what life might be like for the people and animals of the Australian rainforest. The book has a strong visual element, with large collage pictures of the rainforest. Sue wants the children to develop their descriptive writing and decides to use music to help the children go on their own journey through the rainforest. She explains to the children that they will all be going on their own journey.

Sue asks the children to close their eyes and imagine that they are leaving the classroom and travelling across the world to Australia.

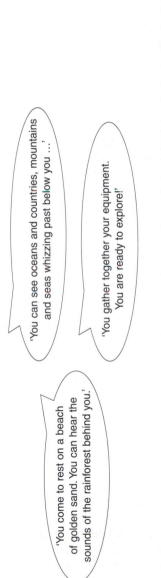

'You can see oceans and countries, mountains and seas whizzing past below you …'

'You gather together your equipment. You are ready to explore!'

'You come to rest on a beach of golden sand. You can hear the sounds of the rainforest behind you.'

While the children have their eyes closed, Sue plays them a piece of aboriginal music that reflects the sounds and feeling of the rainforest. After a few minutes Sue fades the music.

'The rainforest begins to fade and you are flying above rivers and valleys, oceans and mountains again. I am going to count back from ten. When I get to one, you can open your eyes, you will be back in the classroom again.'

The children then talk with their writing partner and tell each other the story of their journey into the rainforest. Some have met people and spoken with them, others have fought with crocodiles and others have just enjoyed the experience of a walk in an unknown environment. All have something they can write about.

If this is the first time you have tried this activity …

- You may find that in the beginning the children find it difficult to keep their eyes closed. They are usually just checking that everyone else has their eyes closed too!
- Create an environment where they feel safe to sit with their eyes closed so they can take part in the visualisation.

4 Writing Aloud – The Role of Oral Rehearsal

Debra Myhill

Introduction

In Chapter 2, we outlined the three different ways in which the Talk to Text project explored how talk supports young children's development as writers. This chapter focuses upon oral rehearsal, or 'write aloud' as we eventually termed it. Recalling Britton's (1970) metaphor of writing as floating 'on a sea of talk', one of the waves of talk which ripples through the process of writing is the interior talk which accompanies the act of writing in most experienced writers. This 'in your head' talk is often reflective talk, evaluating how the unfolding text is matching up to the demands of the task. But the 'in your head' talk is also about trying out words, phrases or sentences, testing how they sound, perhaps trying out alternatives. It is a kind of dialogue between the writer and the emerging text. You might think about what happens when you write. Do you pause mid-sentence to compose the next chunk of text? Do you change words or phrases in your head before you commit them to paper or screen? Do you say your text aloud in your head as you are writing? All of these techniques are typical of mature writers, although they often happen very fast as these processes have become automated with experience. We were interested in investigating whether making this kind of talk more visible in the writing process for young writers might help them to write more confidently and efficiently. In other words, could oral rehearsal, or writing aloud, help to mitigate some of the challenges that writing presents to early years' writers. Very specifically, oral rehearsal is about the movement from ideas in the head to words on the page, the movement from talk to text.

Oral rehearsal in policy documents

The phrase 'oral rehearsal' will not be unfamiliar to most United Kingdom primary school teachers as it is one which was used quite frequently in National Strategy documents in England. A quick search of the Department for Children, Schools and Families (DCSF) Standards website threw up a surprising 453 references to oral rehearsal, most appearing in guidance documentation for teachers. A search through Google shows that this term is used in other countries too, often in relation to second language learning. So you might reasonably expect there to be a clear definition or shared understanding of what oral rehearsal actually is. However, despite the frequency of reference to oral rehearsal, we were unable to find any precise explanation of the term, or any rationale for why its use might be beneficial. It is clear that oral rehearsal is regarded as a teaching strategy, and it is used most frequently in the context of language development. The first 10 references listed after searching the Standards website are all in the context of teaching writing, suggesting that it may have particular significance in this area. The other context in which it recurs is in the teaching of English as an Additional Language (EAL) – we did not explore this area, but our in-service work with teachers since the Talk to Text project finished suggests that oral rehearsal may indeed be a productive strategy to support both EAL learners and those with language difficulties.

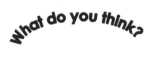

> Is oral rehearsal a term you know? If so, how would you define it?
> Thinking about your current practice in teaching writing, do you make use of oral rehearsal?

So, what can we glean from documentation about the concept of oral rehearsal? Sometimes, tantalisingly little! There are a good number of references to oral rehearsal which simply assume that teachers already know what it is, and refer to the idea of using oral rehearsal without any explanation. However, one cluster of references to oral rehearsal does seem to relate it more specifically to practising written text in oral form before and during writing. The four references below, taken from the Primary National Strategy Literacy Framework (DCSF, 2009) suggest that oral rehearsal in this context means creating opportunities for children to rehearse aloud the phrases and sentences they are going to write before they write them.

Rehearse sentences orally before writing and cumulatively reread while writing. (Year 1 Narrative Unit 1)

Ensure that children are given opportunities to orally rehearse and draft sentences before writing them. (Year 2, 3 and 4 Non-Fiction)

Children orally rehearse their own sentences with a partner before writing. Discuss and make improvement suggestions. (Pupil Writing Targets Year 2)

They follow their story plans, rehearse sentences orally, reread and check as they are writing. (Year 2 Narrative Unit 4)

When we initially set out to investigate oral rehearsal, we assumed that the project team and the teachers involved in the project had a shared understanding of oral rehearsal. But we were mistaken. We were not clear ourselves about whether oral rehearsal was a very general term for talk before writing, including both rehearsing the ideas for a piece of writing and rehearsing how those ideas might be formulated in written text, and the teachers were equally unclear. This was how the term 'write aloud' was born. We decided that it would be most helpful if we restricted the notion of oral rehearsal to rehearsing written text aloud and giving children opportunities to compose text orally, and hear it, before committing it to paper. This contrasts with the more spontaneous, open-ended talk that might be used to generate ideas and support the development of the content for the writing (as described in Chapter 3). To try and provide greater clarity about what we meant by oral rehearsal, we felt that 'write aloud' was a useful phrase to use as it signalled more clearly that children were being asked to speak aloud the text they were going to write. With the children we encouraged them to 'Say it, write it' as can be seen in the poster on p. xii. Most young children understand the difference between reading aloud and reading in your head and writing aloud and writing in your head are mirrors of these processes.

What can research tell us about oral rehearsal?

Perhaps not surprisingly, given the uncertainty in policy documentation that we have noted above, there is very little research specifically on oral rehearsal. Indeed, it is not a term which is widely used in research thinking and when it is used, different researchers use it to mean different things. So, some researchers regard oral rehearsal as a way of helping children to generate the ideas for a piece of writing, often through collaborative or group talk (Cleary, 1996), or through the imaginative talk which can occur informally in play settings (Clark, 2000). Murray suggests that oral rehearsal helps students to 'hear their own voices' (Murray, 1979: 16); although he never explains what he means by oral rehearsal, the fact that saying your text aloud gives you the chance to hear what your text sounds like does seem to have merit. Perhaps drawing on the same idea, Chaffee (1977) argues that oral rehearsal is principally a revision technique, something which happens once a piece of writing is complete: reading the writing aloud helps writers to hear the errors in their text. However, none of these researchers is focusing on oral rehearsal as a strategy; they merely refer to it, almost in passing, and so they provide only a limited insight into its possibilities.

Considering the research on writing development, which we outlined in Chapter 1, it is possible to distinguish at least three aspects of writing development which might be supported by the use of oral rehearsal:

- Developing expertise in the differing language structures of talk and writing
- Reducing the cognitive demand of writing
- Supporting the process of creating text.

We will take each of these aspects in turn and examine it in more depth.

Developing expertise in the differing language structures of talk and writing

In Chapter 1, we explained how young writers have to learn that writing is different from speech and that it makes different demands on how they need to use language to communicate their ideas. The syntactical structures of writing are generally both longer and more complex; writing draws on a vocabulary which often requires a repertoire which extends beyond that of spoken vocabulary, and requires mastery of a whole set of spelling and punctuation conventions which do not exist in talk. We know that experienced writers 'draw on an enlarged vocabulary, a more formalized grammar, a more logically organized rhetorical structure' (Olson, 2006: 140) than is present in talk. In essence, these differences relate to the fact that there is a range of socially accepted conventions for writing and that speech and writing occur in different contexts. Crystal (1995: 291) notes the many contrasts that occur as a consequence of the phonic nature of talk and the graphic nature of writing, including: the presence of contextual cues in speech which are absent in writing; the permanence of writing set against the transience of talk; and the communicative power of intonation and non-verbal gestures in talk which are hard to replicate in writing. Olson recognises that these contrasts pose an explicit learning challenge to children because 'a speaker has a richer range of resources at hand than does a writer; writers must invent or learn lexical and grammatical functions to compensate for such paralinguistic features as facial expression and tone of voice' (Olson, 2006: 140).

Oral rehearsal may be particularly helpful in enabling young writers to develop understanding of these differences between speech and writing. Oral rehearsal gives them the opportunity to 'write aloud' before they begin writing on paper, so that they are able to rehearse written structures which differ from the more natural spoken structures. Young writers are then able to hear written phrases or sentences spoken aloud, by themselves, their peers or their teacher and can develop increasing discrimination between talk and writing.

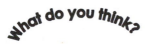

Have you noticed ways in which the writers in your class are influenced by structures they use in their talk?

Reducing the cognitive demand of writing

We also noted in Chapter 1 just how difficult writing is as a cognitive activity and the considerable demand it makes on cognitive resources – remember that Kellogg (2008) claimed writing was as mentally difficult as playing chess! Writing makes particular demands on our working memory, the temporary information store in our brain, because as we write we are trying to juggle multiple sets of information and thinking. As we write, working memory is constantly switching attention between 'language generation' to convey ideas in words, and 'planning ideas, reviewing ideas, and coordinating all three processes', as well as 'maintaining multiple representations of the text in working memory' (Kellogg, 2008: 3). Writing is the ultimate multi-tasking activity! Experienced writers, as are all of you reading this book, are simultaneously juggling what they want to communicate in writing with how best to say it – including holding an overall shape of the whole text in their head while developing the text clause by clause, checking as the text is unfolding that it is going in the right direction or questioning whether the planned direction needs altering, and judging whether they are providing enough information for the reader as well as searching for the right word or image. And, as we explained in Chapter 1, if you are a beginning writer you also have to manage holding your pen and shaping letters, trying to spell words you haven't written before, and remembering the conventions of punctuation – processes which are largely automatic for older, more experienced, writers. To make matters worse if you are in the early years, your working memory is smaller than it is when you are older, so you are in effect trying to do more with less. It is not surprising, then, that for young writers the effort involved in both transcription and text generation 'can overload their ability to hold much information in memory' (Shanahan, 2006: 173).

Teachers often comment, with disappointment, that children's writing sometimes does not match up to the quality of their ideas expressed orally: indeed, this is a comment made by early years teachers which is frequently echoed in the secondary school, especially with regard to weaker writers and boys. Research provides evidence which suggests that this mismatch is attributable to the cognitive demand of writing and the burden that writing places on working memory. Bourdin and Fayol (1994, 2002) and Fayol (1991) compared the cognitive effort involved in creating oral stories and written stories in both young children and adults. They found that, regardless of age, writing made more demand on mental resources than talk. In adult writers, although the physical process of writing and the processes of spelling, punctuation and retrieving vocabulary from the memory make very limited demands on working memory because they have become virtually automatised, high demands are still made of the working memory because writers have developed increased sophistication and expectation of what the writing should achieve and because they are often composing text, and evaluating and generating ideas simultaneously. For young writers, though, the effort involved in transcription, before it becomes an automated process, is particularly significant. The need of young writers to devote mental attention to transcription gets in the way of their being able to think about the writing as a whole or even the writing created so far. Fayol (1991) argues that this cognitive load accounts for the fact that oral storytelling by young children is often better than their written composition.

Given what we know, then, about the mental demands of writing, oral rehearsal can be used as a strategy to reduce the burden of writing, freeing up valuable mental resource to think about other aspects of writing. Psychologists talk about reducing 'cognitive load' by partitioning attention to different aspects of a task so that everything doesn't need to be done at once (Kellogg, 2008). As teachers you already know this, even if you may not have expressed it in this way. When you tell children just to put down the first sound of a spelling they don't know and a line and come back to it later, you are reducing the cognitive load; when you scribe for a child, you are reducing the cognitive load; when you write suggestions for the vocabulary for a writing task on the board, you are reducing the cognitive load. By asking children to orally rehearse a sentence or phrase before writing it, you are also reducing the cognitive load because the child has to retrieve the ideas and vocabulary and shape them into a syntactically appropriate form before attempting the challenge of transcription. It may be that oral rehearsal also reduces the cognitive load because of the impact on memory of saying something aloud. This is rather like the way many of us when given a telephone number to write down repeat it aloud first and then repeat it as we write it – the process helps us to hold it in our memory. Hayes draws attention to the articulatory rehearsal process, a sub-component of working memory which is akin to speaking to oneself, and which 'has the effect of increasing the time that material can be maintained in the short term store' (2006: 29): oral rehearsal is a form of speaking to oneself.

Supporting the process of creating text: from talk to text

So far, we have considered how oral rehearsal can support young writers in distinguishing between spoken and written language characteristics, and in reducing the mental demand of writing. A final way in which we think it can help young writers is in being a bridge from ideas to text, literally supporting the transition from talk to text. If you recall the model of writing described in Chapter 1, there were three stages which researchers have argued make up the process of writing – planning, translating (which we called 'creating text') and reviewing. Curiously, given that from a classroom perspective we know how hard young children find the translating, or creating text, stage, there has been much more research into planning and reviewing, than into the translating stage. Researchers have tended to assume that putting ideas into words and writing them down is straightforward, compared with the problem of coming up with ideas in the first place and the problem of making evaluative judgements about what you have written. In other words, creating text has been regarded largely as an unproblematic and linear process of the linguistic conversion of ideas in the head to words on the page. Research has also tended to assume that producing written text draws on the same resources as producing spoken text; so models of language production such as those proposed by Bock and Levelt (1994) and Bock (1995), which focus upon the mechanisms by which a speaker converts thoughts into spoken utterances, have been used as an appropriate way to explain the movement from thoughts to written text.

But we feel these are problematic assumptions, especially for writers in the early years. If we know that writing for young children is particularly mentally demanding, and that they have to learn NOT to write as they talk, then the process of moving from spoken ideas to those ideas being well expressed in writing is no mean feat. Moving from talk to text is not a simple process of linguistic conversion or translation but 'a transformative act' (Myhill, 2009b), a creative process of finding not just words to express ideas but the right words in the right order. Not only do young writers need to learn not to write in the same way that they talk, but they need to create and shape phrases, images and sentences to do justice to the ideas in their head. Increasingly, as they become more experienced and more of the spelling and punctuation aspects of writing are automatised, this shaping of ideas into text becomes more important. Oral rehearsal can be a strategy for testing out or modelling written ideas before writing them down, akin to the internal 'in the head' rehearsal more common in older writers. You might want to think about what you do when you write. As I write this, I tend to pause before the start of a sentence or a phrase and run through possibilities in my head. I do this particularly at 'sticky corners' when I am stuck or when I am unsure about what to write next. Then I often have a little burst of writing several sentences without stopping.

How do you write? Do you ever talk aloud as you write, or are you aware of talking in your head as you write? Do you stop mid-sentence and work out what you are going to say next?
Do you share these writing experiences with the children in your class?

To summarise, then, we believe that there are good reasons why oral rehearsal can be a supportive strategy for developing young writers. Indeed, oral rehearsal may have a particular role to play in supporting the process of creating text by enabling a first stage of formulation of ideas which is undertaken orally, and is then followed by the written formulation. This may reduce the cognitive load incurred by writing because the phrase or sentence has been generated and shaped orally at the point at which the writer begins the transcription process. Thus oral rehearsal supports the transition from talk to text by reducing the mental demand of writing, by making explicit the differing demands of spoken and written text and by allowing writers to test out various possibilities before committing their words to paper. We think that oral rehearsal is the 'ideal bridge' between the creative, spontaneous, content-forming talk used to generate ideas and the more ordered, scripted nature of writing.

Exploring oral rehearsal in the classroom

In deciding to encourage the use of oral rehearsal to support writing, we were being very exploratory and unsure of what might happen – and the very positive response by the teachers to the impact of oral rehearsal was one of the surprises of the project. The teachers were themselves surprised by the results. One teacher noted that she 'couldn't believe how imaginative they have been' and noted that even low-attaining writers had improved their writing. She attributed this improvement to the fact that oral rehearsal allows the children 'to think about it before writing it down' and that oral rehearsal makes it 'easier to change it [writing] in talk than when it has been written down'. Sometimes oral rehearsal appeared to enable writers to write more or to attempt writing with more confidence.

One feature which clearly distinguished oral rehearsal from other talk used in the writing classroom was that it sounded different. It did not sound like natural talk: the pitch and intonation altered from the rhythms and intonations of natural speech to a slower, more deliberate delivery which was more like reading aloud than conversation. You might say that the nature of this talk reflected the idea of 'rehearsal'. To try and show clearly where oral rehearsal was occurring, all examples of oral rehearsal in the extracts we use in the following sections will be represented in bold print.

Using oral rehearsal to compose aloud

Young children (and many adults too!) can often be heard vocalising what they write as they write it as a very natural and instinctive way of tackling writing. When children are encouraged to vocalise their text, as oral rehearsal, before writing it down, they are, in effect, composing aloud. Such oral rehearsal may well be a precursor to the internal mental rehearsal common in more experienced writers. This tended to happen mostly as an individual activity, even when children were supposed to be working with partners, as though it was more of a dialogue between the writer and the unfolding text rather than talk between peers. You can see this in the extract below where Kate and her partner are supposed to be working together, but her partner simply gets on with what he is doing. Even Kate's comment, 'Yes, that's OK', draws no response and may be a dialogue with herself rather than with her uninterested partner. The teacher's intervention is important because it gives her an opportunity to repeat her sentence which she does with greater confidence and fluency than on the first occasion.

Kate   [Partner writing his letter throughout. Kate sits chewing her pencil and looks as though she is thinking what to write.] **Dear dad ...** [Long pause – hears other children's talk off – then starts to rehearse beneath her breath. The full sentence is not wholly audible.] **Mum ... won't let ... me play football ... she'll let Laura ... it's not fair.** Yes, that's OK. [Partner does not respond.]

Teacher   [Coming across from another table] Can you say what your first sentence is going to be?

Kate   Yes.

Teacher   Tell me what it is then.

Kate   **Mum won't let ... won't let me play football but** and then I'm going to do a full stop alright **but she will let Laura play tennis. It's not fair.**

The little mid-sentence aside, about using a full stop, is in a conversational voice directed at the teacher and when you hear Kate speaking the shift from the oral rehearsal to this aside is very clear. It is an interesting aside as it may be that Kate has realised that you can't indicate punctuation marks when you say your text aloud; or it may simply reflect her knowledge that the teacher will want to know she has not forgotten about the punctuation (even if she is putting her full stop in the wrong place!)

Using oral rehearsal to practise shaping sentences

Sometimes the oral rehearsal we witnessed was much more about practising and rehearsing emerging sentences. These embryo sentences were re-phrased or amended orally. In one classroom, the children were given the task of writing an instructional text on how to write an instructional text. The children were asked to work in pairs, though again this was not always what they did. In the extract below, Libby reminds Robert that they are supposed to be working and starts to rehearse her sentence, but Robert never contributes to the 'dialogue'. Libby's oral rehearsal tests out different possibilities – she replaces 'say' with 'put', and she refines 'start of a instruction' to 'start of a sentence', then reverts to her original in the final completed sentence.

Libby   [Libby grabs Robert and directs him to the task.]
Come on, Robert … Don't say please, don't say .. in … in don't put
please in instructions in … at … in .. the … um .. the … um … at the …
start of … a … a … instruction … start of a sentence.
Don't put please at the start of a instruction.

Using oral rehearsal to foster peer support during writing

Even when asked to work in pairs, children do not always actively engage in working together, and there were numerous examples in these writing classrooms of pair work involving relatively little peer interaction. However, there were also numerous occasions when the pair work was supportive and constructive. One set of examples of oral rehearsal occurred when one child in a pair helped the other child with his/her writing. Both children were focused on one child's text, but one child asked questions or offered suggestions to the other child to enable him/her to continue the writing.

In the example below, Kylie and Jack are both writing a first person piece from the viewpoint of a rainforest animal in danger of extinction. This has followed work which the class has shared together on rainforest animals and the environmental issues which are threatening them. Kylie starts a sentence but her long pause suggests she is unsure where to take it next, so Jack intervenes by trying to get her to think about the task and why her animal is becoming extinct, using the prompt sheet the teacher has given them. Kylie then orally rehearses a possible answer to Jack's question and again gets stuck at the point of completion. The supportiveness of the pair work here is underlined by their shared amusement at her 'forgetting the last bit'. Then Jack offers her a possible model, orally rehearsing it to her – you can see clearly how Jack switches from the oral rehearsal of 'All the trees have been chopped down so I can't live in the shade' to more typical dialogue with Kylie, telling her that his suggestion is just an example ('things like that') and that is the kind of thing she needs to do.

Kylie   … umm .. **In the forest** … [long pause]

Jack   Why are you becoming extinct? [reading from his sheet, then turns to look at her]

Kylie   **Because they're chopping down all the leaves … and the trees and stuff** … **and … and** … [pause]

Jack   Have you forgotten the last bit? [laughs]

Kylie   [laughs] Yes.

Jack   So … **All the trees have been chopped down so I can't live in the shade** … and things like that. That's the thing you've ….

Kylie   **They're chopping all the leaves down and ...**

Jack   [Whispers to prompt] ... **and there's no shade left.**

Kylie   **and there's no shade left.**

Looking at this exchange closely is interesting because you can see that peer-supported oral rehearsal like this is far more than one peer giving the other a sentence to write. Jack's sentence reformulates slightly Kylie's initial attempt ('Because they're chopping down all the leaves' becomes 'All the trees have been chopped down') but Kylie's retains her version when she completes her sentence. The oral rehearsal process happening here is not mere imitation.

Using oral rehearsal for shared composition

Another cluster of oral rehearsal interactions also demonstrate partners working together constructively but in this case working more collaboratively and equally towards the creation of a piece of writing. In the first example below, Tim and Alice are each writing their own version of a narrative, based on a story they have shared in class. Before they begin composing their text, Alice reminds them both what the content of the sentence will be addressing – this is very much talk to generate ideas. But then, with a very obvious alteration in intonation, she rehearses the first part of the sentence, followed by both of them rehearsing the next chunk of the sentence in unison. Finally, Alice completes it and they both turn to write the sentence down.

Alice   [To her partner; spoken as though it is a framing of an idea rather than a rehearsal.] It's going to go to the house the same day as he wrote the letter in the afternoon.

Alice   [Said very deliberately] **He delivered ... the ... the letter to the giant ...** [small pause]

Tim   **the same day he wrote it** ⎱
                         ⎰ in unison
Alice   **the same day he wrote it** ⎰

Alice   **in the afternoon.** [They both write.]

In another example, May and Luke are working together on devising an instructional text providing guidance on how to write. This pair are confident in using oral rehearsal to test out sentences and May initiates an oral rehearsal sequence by asking Luke for an idea to help her finish. The next four exchanges illustrate May and Luke alternately orally rehearsing different possibilities for the sentence, making small changes each time, until May arrives at the one she is happy to use.

May   [To partner] What could I use for my last idea?

Luke   **Look at what you're writing. Look … at … what …**

May   [moves to start writing] **Think what you're going to write** [looks at Luke]

Luke   **Look what you're writing. Look at what you write.**

May   **Think what you are going to do.**

It is also interesting to notice here that in Luke's second interaction with May, he rehearses his sentence twice, trying out two different possibilities for the verb phrase.

This exploration of how young writers use oral rehearsal has demonstrated its potential for supporting the challenging transition from talk to text. In particular, the way that oral rehearsal enables the move from expressing ideas for writing through natural talk to articulating the possible written text orally is most important. We have here only considered oral rehearsal as the precursor to writing acting as the bridge from oral to written, but it may be that we should extend how we think of oral rehearsal to include reading written text aloud so that you can hear how your writing sounds. This could happen both as a planned strategy when the piece of writing is complete, or as a strategy which individuals use during writing to help them continue. Pausing during writing to re-read the text that has already been written is a practice adopted by most experienced writers, and in a different way it may well help beginner writers, particularly at the level of phrase and sentence composition. Additionally, we did not look specifically at oral rehearsal as a strategy to support children with English as an additional language or with specific language difficulties, but our in-service work with teachers and with advisory bodies since the project suggests that this might be a very rich vein to tap. So, to conclude, we feel that, as yet, the full potential of oral rehearsal has not been realised and we would encourage you to experiment creatively with the strategy in your own writing classrooms.

Teaching activities for oral rehearsal

The teachers on the project tried out many ways of introducing write aloud into their lessons. These worked best when the write aloud activity followed on from the idea generation. In these cases it facilitated the difficult shift from talking about ideas to getting them down on paper. In Chapter 3, where the focus is on idea generation, a lesson was described where the teacher had used Conscience Alley as a way of generating ideas about what the baby bird, Billywise, and his mother would say as he was plucking up courage to fly. Here the talk activity in which the children actually took part in and spoke the different words in the Conscience Alley game fed naturally into the writing activity.

Furthermore, the teacher's use of speech bubbles for the writing helped support this transition.

One of the most surprising, yet most successful, lessons was one where some form of 'magic pencil' was involved. (A lesson plan based on this idea is contained in the section on plans for write aloud, p. 100). The first lesson using this idea took place during the pilot year but is worth describing in full as it exemplifies how successful this idea can be. We had had the idea of setting up a fantasy situation, giving children a blank sheet of paper and asking them to 'read' and then write over the words that they saw. Drawing on young children's willingness to suspend reality, this was a huge success.

A letter from the man in the moon

At the start of the lesson Rachael told the children that she had received a very special package with pictures on the front. She showed a large brown envelope with pictures of moons and stars on it. She wondered out loud what might be inside. One child called Zayn suggested a present. Another child said 'something for the class'. Rachael took out a blank piece of paper. A child called out that it could be an invitation. Rachael reminded the class that they had been reading a book about someone who holds a birthday party. And the children guess it is an invitation from the man in the moon.

Rachael then introduced the idea of a magical pen, which writes in invisible ink. All the children seemed transfixed by this and she had their full attention. The children became very enthusiastic about reading the invisible writing. She said they must think hard about what the man in the moon had written. She pointed to invisible words and prompted children to read them by giving the initial letter sounds. She encouraged them to think about the man in the moon and, for example, what time would he have his party?

Rachael then showed the class that in the package there were a whole lot of envelopes with pictures on them and a child's name on each one so they each got to open their own invitation and found it written in invisible writing. One child immediately began to read out his invisible invitation to the child sitting next to him. Another child read his out to the Teaching Assistant. A number of children claimed straight away that they could see the invisible writing.

Rachael then split the class into pairs and instructed them to read the invitation out to their partner and then swap over. She didn't tell them at this stage that they would have to write over it. At first some children were confused and said they couldn't see anything but soon most got into the idea and were enthusiastic to have a go at reading.

After a while Rachael stopped the talk and told the class that they needed to be able to keep their invitations and so would have to write over them. She explained tracing over the invisible words with a pencil. Some children seemed to write fluently and others looked as though they were tracing over writing.

At the end of the lesson, they returned to the carpet to read out the writing they had traced over. Zayn read his out first. Rachael praised his writing.

Katie read out hers and Rachael asked her if she found it easy or hard. Amelia said it was hard because she had so much information in her head. Ellen read hers out and said she found it easy because she 'looked carefully and saw every single bit'.

Following the lesson the researcher talked to both the teacher and head teacher who had been observing the lesson. They both felt that it went very well. They were both very impressed by Zayn's performance. He was a child with behavioural and learning difficulties and this was the first time he had really engaged with a writing task or done any writing. He usually got very upset when asked to write. The head teacher said she cried when she saw how well he was doing. Subsequent lessons of this kind also proved to be very liberating for those children who normally struggled with their writing. (Adapted from field notes for this observation.)

The idea of a magic pencil was taken on by other teachers in the project and some found it very helpful. You can read in two of the Interlude sections in this book Rachael's and another teacher's thoughts about this strategy. Not all attempts to use it were successful. Looking at the videos of these lessons it seems that what made this first lesson successful was that each child had their own letter and Rachael made it clear that they were the ones who could read what was written. Where teachers just produced one single class blank sheet of paper to introduce the idea it was more difficult. It also seemed important for the teacher to make clear that the particular child could decide what was written rather than that there is one right answer that the child has somehow to find.

The idea of the magic pencil developed over the course of the project. As well as the idea of a magic implement for capturing invisible writing, it became a strategy that children could use whenever they were thinking about what to write. Each teacher developed the strategy in a slightly different way and different classes used different ideas such as a magic finger, writing on their hands (of course with invisible ink), writing in the air, and so on, as ways of practising the writing before using a real pencil or pen.

Summary of points for the class teacher 🔲

➢ Use teacher modelling to make sure that children understand how to rehearse sentences orally. Oral rehearsal activities such as 'invisible writing' or 'magic pencil' work best when children have seen the ideas demonstrated first.

➢ Make the terms 'write aloud' and 'writing aloud' part of your vocabulary for teaching writing so that the idea of oral rehearsal becomes embedded within children's writing practices.

(Continued)

(Continued)

➤ Follow talk activities which promote idea generation with an oral rehearsal activity to help actively bridge the transition between talk and text. So, for example, you could move from a role play where children take on the roles of characters from a book you have been sharing, into an 'invisible writing' activity which invites children to orally rehearse a letter from the character they had role-played.

➤ Follow oral rehearsal activities with talk tasks which encourage reflection on writing so that creating text is accompanied by discussion about effectiveness. So, for example, after an oral rehearsal activity where children have orally rehearsed a story to a toy, they switch to working with a peer and orally rehearse their text to each other. The partner offers comments about words or phrases which s/he particularly likes or suggestions about words or phrases which might be altered.

➤ Make use of digital voice recording technology to support oral rehearsal. Basic digital voice recorders which can be replayed instantly through a USB port allow you to share children's oral rehearsal. There are some commercial products which are excellent for facilitating oral rehearsal: such as the Chatterbox which allows you to record short extracts of talk from lots of children and could be used for rehearsing sentence possibilities around the class, or Big Points which allows children to record oral rehearsals and play them back instantly. There are many of these kinds of products available, including talking photo albums, instant replay microphones for children and talking postcards. To see products of this kind, have a look at the Talk Time section on www.tts-group.co.uk.

➤ Encourage higher quality collaborative writing through the use of oral rehearsal. Genuine collaborative writing is hard to foster, but oral rehearsal makes visible the process of composing and makes it easier for partners to share the process. In this context, consider giving writers more collaborative writing tasks where two writers work together to compose a single text, rather than the more common strategy of two writers working together on their two separate texts.

Suggested further reading

Dyson, A.H. (2000) 'Writing and the Sea of Voices: Oral Language In, Around and About Writing', in R. Indrisano and J.R. Squires (eds) *Perspectives on*

Writing: Research Theory and Practice. Newark, DL: International Reading Association. pp. 45–65.

Parr, J. Jesson, R. and McNaughton, S. (2009) 'Agency and Platform: the Relationships Between Talk and Writing', in R. Beard, D. Myhill, J. Riley and M. Nystrand (eds) *The Sage Handbook of Writing Development.* London: SAGE. pp. 246–59.

Interlude 2

Using Write Aloud in the Classroom

Rachael Milsom

Class teacher

Starting the pilot for the Talk to Text project in 2005 during my Newly Qualified Teacher (NQT) year, was not only beneficial for the children I was teaching, but it became a confidence boost for me professionally. I found myself with a new bank of fresh, exciting ideas and enthusiasm to get into the classroom to try them out.

The area I found most interesting was 'write aloud'. Although I took the project on fully in my classroom I have to confess that write aloud was the area I was most interested in and where I felt I could have the most fun, developing my imaginative teaching methods. I was eager to investigate ways children could have more fun with writing and give them the freedom to be able to write for pleasure without being scared of the constraints such as good ideas, handwriting and spelling.

I often used the suggestions of talk partners, puppets and role play during my lessons but there was one aspect of the project that I feel made a significant breakthrough with my class and truly made writing enjoyable. Throughout our meetings during the project, the words 'invisible writing' came up and although sceptical at first, I was curious to see how this would work in the classroom.

I was teaching a boy top-heavy class, many being summer born with lots being quite hesitant to share ideas or put pen to paper. They were all keen to talk, but getting them to put their imaginative ideas down on paper was often tricky. Some were just reluctant, others would give it a go for a sentence or two and there were a few who refused point blank to write.

One of my most successful lessons (and judged by the teaching awards in 2006, see p. 178) was based on the story of *The Magical Bicycle* (by B. Doherty and C. Birmingham). Off I went, collecting resources for an invisible writing lesson; magic wand, magic box, gold pencils, blank spell sheets.

After reading the story, we decided that we wanted a spell to give us the power to learn how to ride a bike successfully. But what would it say? (This is where the bag of tricks came in!) The magical horse from the story had kindly sent us spells to read, but unfortunately they were written in invisible ink and could only be seen by the children. They had miniature magnifying glasses in order to read what their spell said and after a few baffled looks (as if to imply I may well and truly have lost the plot!), discussions amongst themselves and a modelling session using my own spell, there were suddenly squeals of excitement. I describe it as the 'emperor's new clothes syndrome'. Children who had previously not been in on the magic were suddenly starting to say things like 'I can see it' and 'Can I read you mine?'

Nobody wanted to admit they hadn't got a spell on their page and even those most sceptical were desperate to share what their magic writing said. After sharing some of our spells, I knew the most crucial point was coming up … the part where I asked them to do the dreaded 'W' word … WRITE!! This was the part where I expected groans of the usual 'I can't do it' and where I thought all the magic would leave the classroom as quickly as it had came. To continue the magic for a little longer, we turned ordinary writing pencils into gold ones (using a very loud 'ABRACADABRA' and a cleverly fashioned, double-ended washing powder box!) and off they went.

To my surprise, as all I was asking them to do was simply to 'trace' over their magic spell (remember, these pieces of paper were blank), the pressure of thinking up ideas had gone. They had already 'read' their spell out loud to others and so using their gold pencils to 'go over' the writing was the easy bit, and the best part is that lower or higher ability, all children completed their spell at their level.

Needless to say, invisible writing became a feature in my class for special writing. Tempting as it was to use it all the time, I kept it to maybe once a term. The children remembered these lessons for a long time and talked about them throughout the year. I loved the buzz that came from the children and the fact that they were writing for pleasure and found it fun – exactly what I had set out to do.

Introduction

In this chapter we take a break from exploring the three strategic elements of using talk to support writing to look at the impact that this talk may have on the child's writing. We have placed this chapter here as it is those two elements described in the previous two chapters, idea generation and oral rehearsal, that mainly feed into the actual writing that the child produces.

There is a strong tradition within primary classrooms of valuing interactive, talk-based environments; from circle time to group work, from talk partners to hot-seating, teachers are familiar with the link that is made between talking and learning. The oral skills that children develop prior to formal schooling are viewed as a resource to support the development of the social, cognitive and conceptual aspects of the curriculum. The use of talk as a key instructional tool for supporting emergent writers is also well established practice in early years classrooms. While there is an obvious relationship between speaking and writing, as explained in Chapter 1, writing cannot be seen as merely speech written down. The Talk to Text project sought to explore how different talk activities impacted in different ways on the complex activity of writing. Two of these strategies have already been explored in previous chapters: talk to generate ideas and talk as oral rehearsal. Distinguishing between these two strategies highlights the complexity of the task that young writers face; generating ideas can motivate and enthuse children, giving them something they might wish to communicate through writing, but framing this enthusiasm and imaginative content into well crafted sentences poses a different set of problems. The project was concerned to develop strategies that recognised that talk activities needed to be aimed more strategically at the nature of the writing process itself, and to develop an understanding of these strategies through the application of research techniques.

This chapter moves on from the talk activities to consider the patterns of talk observed and the writing produced and to try to tease out how the classroom talk opportunities that teachers have so carefully integrated into their teaching become words on the page. In order to tell this story we will firstly look at the talk patterns we observed across all the classes taking part, then take a focused look at two lessons from the project. Both these lessons have already been referred to in the two previous chapters. The aim is not to present these lessons as exemplars or models of good practice, although each do contain examples of good practice, rather the purpose is to consider the resulting texts in the light of the classroom talk that produced them, in order to develop an understanding of the relationship between classroom talk and the texts children write. Research provides a second eye in the classroom revealing through analysis aspects of the classroom not visible to the teacher. Reflecting on what this analysis reveals is in no way intended to be a critique of the teaching we observed, indeed teachers were integrating into their own practice strategies that had originated from the research context and it is these strategies that are being explored. The value of this second eye in enabling teachers to explore their own practice was explored in Chapter 2, here the intention is to use the techniques of the researcher to make the invisible visible.

Capturing classroom talk

As part of the research project the teachers videoed their own writing lessons across an academic year. This involved capturing the whole-class interactive sessions, generally at the beginning of a lesson, then focusing the camera on a pair of children engaged in talking and writing activities at tables to pick up their talk and interaction as they wrote. A third type of talk, often part of the plenary, included whole-class episodes that focused on reflective talk about the qualities and features of the text and the act of producing it; a form of talk that is discussed in Chapter 6. The cameras became permanent features in our classrooms so the children became familiarised with having them around, never really knowing whether they were in use or not. Six focus children were observed from each class representing a balance of gender and achievement. Chapter 2 explored in more detail how we collected our data, not in terms of a formal account of our methodology but as a means of helping teachers engage in reflective practice themselves. In total we recorded 24 one-hour lessons and from these recordings we were able to complete a detailed analysis of the talk in which the children engaged when they were working in pairs.

We analysed the talk in order to understand not what the talk was about, because this was clearly going to differ from lesson to lesson, but to understand what kind of talk was taking place and especially to consider how this might support writing. A lengthy and time-consuming analysis process revealed three key features of the talk we observed: strategic talk, evaluative talk and constructive talk.

Strategic talk

We defined this as 'A strategy is originated by the writer which has the intention of having an effect on the user's writing'. It is essentially forward thinking often used when the child is actually writing. Strategic talk captured all those examples of children adopting a strategy. A key feature of this talk is that often what is being said is a verbal representation of the text itself. Thus strategic talk largely includes examples of children actively engaged in one strategy or another to support the writing itself. This might be the conscious use of strategies such as oral rehearsal or magic pencil that originated in the ideas developed in the project itself. It also included examples of strategies the children naturally and perhaps habitually employed while writing. For example, strategic talk included re-reading text in order to generate new ideas or asking their partner or the teacher for help with ideas. A common feature of their talk was the speaking of text quietly to themselves as they wrote; this was not the direct use of oral rehearsal but seemed to support writers in monitoring where they were in a sentence as they wrote.

Less frequent, but still evident, were oral attempts to re-form sentences during writing to hear the difference in emphasis and effect. Encouraging children to generate different versions of the same idea or sentence could itself be developed into a formal talk activity focusing on orally rehearsing a variety of possible sentences in order to select a preferred option – discussing why one sentence might be preferable to another presents a further talk opportunity focusing on evaluating the quality and effect of the text produced, a feature of classroom talk that is discussed below.

While much of this talk focused on the generating, marshalling and shaping of ideas a considerable amount focused on the secretarial aspects of writing, especially spelling. This might include individual efforts at sounding out words phonetically or asking other children how to spell a word. A recurring theme in any research into children and writing is the priority children give to surface features such as neatness and accuracy. While no teacher would consider neatness and accuracy unimportant, the extent to which it can eclipse the attention children give to the content, purpose and impact of what they write is striking. This begs the question of where such attitudes come from and the extent to which pedagogy informs and reinforces these perceptions.

Strategic talk is difficult to illustrate because it is defined more by what the children are doing as they talk than with what they are saying, but its key purpose seems to be forward thinking; that is, consciously attempting to move the writing activity on through a strategic focus on the writing process itself.

Evaluative talk

Strategic talk is forward thinking and concerned with the writing process; evaluative talk, on the other hand, involves reflecting on the talk or the text itself and this category of talk included examples of children commenting on their own or their partners' ideas or writing. These were both positive and negative and could be encouraging, critiquing or dispiriting. Echoing the examples of strategic talk, a considerable proportion of these evaluative comments relate to the secretarial aspects of writing and reveal children valuing 'how much' and 'how neat' over 'how interesting'. Evaluating the neatness of writing is generally informed by the size of the writing – small is neater and attempts at joining letters are valued even when it doesn't improve readability. These findings will come as no surprise to primary teachers but indicate that creating opportunities for evaluative talk that broadens thinking of what 'good' writing is might help develop an understanding that goes beyond the surface features of a text.

Nevertheless there are examples of children evaluating ideas and content and several of these examples included the positing and accepting of the ideas and vocabulary offered by a partner.

Year 2 class writing route directions round the town in pairs:

David   Around the … around the cottage

Amy   What's the cottage … we have to use a describing word

David   OK – I'll do it on the back [turns paper over]

David   Around the …

Amy   [whispers a suggestion]

David   Yes!!! Thatched … You stole that from them

This paired construction of a sentence was common, and was often formalised in classroom practice by encouraging children to write a single text between them. There are several possible gains in adopting this strategy; the children may have to use linguistic terminology in order to communicate their intentions, here Amy refers to 'describing words', although the emphasis on 'we have to' indicates that the use of the adjective may be more to please the teacher than to satisfy personal writing intentions. By sharing the scribing, the cognitive demands of the task can be reduced in turns by each member of the partnership, thus freeing attention for the generation and shaping of ideas. This co-construction of a sentence means children may have to choose between different possible sentence constructions and vocabulary choices, thus emphasising the idea of writing as a design activity. David's remark about stealing ideas is especially revealing of how classroom values are internalised. The common teacher stipulation that 'I want to hear your own ideas here' or the student complaint 'Miss she's copying me' are all reminders of the way classrooms can mitigate against the idea of collaborative learning. The irony here is that arguably David has just 'stolen' 'thatched' from Amy.

Evaluative talk also included examples of children articulating and evaluating the suitability and phrasing of ideas and explaining their own thinking.

Year 2 class writing about keeping safe on the beach using a picture as a prompt:

Tim   Which bit do you think is the best?

Alice   Actually I think the headlines like 'Keeping yourself safe in the sun' and then like the sea because the sea can be dangerous too.

In this task the pair had come up with lots of do's and don'ts for keeping safe on the beach then redesigned the list under different headings relating to the sea, the sun and the cliffs. When evaluating their writing it was this design feature Alice comments on rather than any phrase or idea. The multiple nature of the evaluative skills required to produce an effective text is evident, children need to evaluate not only the quality of their ideas but also their suitability, their phrasing, their ordering and the emphasis they require. There is scope through evaluative talk to make these choices explicit.

Talk then can be strategic and address the problem of how to complete the writing task, and it can be evaluative and address the problem of judging the value and purpose of what is written. The third form of talk we identified is concerned with the constructive properties of talk itself in terms of the way it supports learning.

Constructive talk

If strategic talk focuses on the writing process and evaluative talk focuses on the written text then constructive talk focuses on the social and communicative possibilities of talk. These statements are very much concerned with the current and ongoing support that children give each other and also the support offered by the teacher, including the child's response to this support. This might be talk in which children share ideas or discuss the task; constructive talk is highly interactive and full of examples of the way ideas are generated through interaction, growing and taking shape through the talk itself. This happened both in terms of the generating of ideas for writing and at the level of orally rehearsing sentences which were sometimes shaped through paired interaction as illustrated in the previous chapter. This pattern of talk buys into Vygotskian principles of the value of co-constructed learning and learning as a social endeavour which has been very much at the heart of education theory and practice in recent years. Generally constructive talk takes place in extended episodes of interaction which include examples of negotiation, speculation and prompting and is typified by statements such as:

- How about if we …
- Why have you done it like that?
- Tell me what you've put

- Listen to this

- I've done it like this, look

- What if we use your bit here?

- How shall we finish it then?

- No not that … what was that last thing you said?

It is best illustrated by extended examples. In the beach safety lesson a pair of children spend a long time discussing a figure on a cliff and the chances of him falling or jumping off. Several flights of fancy are explored, such as whether he is a diver or maybe he is fishing, ideas that belong in the narrative genre rather than an information leaflet. As they struggle to express this in a sentence the formal tone for the beginning of this text they are writing starts to inform their thinking. (A full transcript for the beginning of this interchange can be found in Chapter 3.) The possibility of someone jumping off a cliff is questioned by Crystal who suggests he won't jump off because he could walk down, but the danger of the cliff still needs to be represented and finally Jamie suggests 'Don't play football on the cliffs' Crystal thinks 'side of a cliff' is better but the final text reads 'Don't play football on the edge of a cliff.' This sets the tone for lots of examples using the imperative 'don't' until, prompted by the teacher, Jamie suggests they should start their sentences in a different way and through talk, the pair struggle to represent the same ideas in the positive. This struggle is informed by the belief that the repetition of 'don't' is an undesirable feature of the writing. In this example the talk is addressing several things at once: the generation, suitability, phrasing and crafting of ideas, and illustrates the complexity of the task young writers face. It demonstrates, however, the generative possibilities of talk for identifying and engaging with the nature of the problem.

Patterns of talk

Taking the whole sample together and looking especially at the talk generated in pairs when the children were working on their writing at tables, the pattern of talk revealed that 57% of talk was strategic, 14% was evaluative and 29% was constructive. This highlights how little of the talk focused on the written text itself and suggests that generating talk activities that support evaluative talk in the context of writing might prove helpful. This may be especially valuable given the reluctance children have for revising their work as a post writing activity when they consider the task has been completed.

That almost one third of all the talk observed is constructive might be seen as a positive outcome for a set of strategies aimed to develop the possibilities of shared talk in shaping learning and supporting writing. Considering these findings in the

Table 5.1   How achievement level influences talk patterns

Achievement	Strategic	Evaluative	Constructive
High	40%	42%	60%
Average	30%	28%	20%
Low	30%	30%	18%

light of how this reflects the different achievement levels represented by these children however gives pause for thought.

High achievers are engaging more in all of the different kinds of talk observed but are very much more likely to be engaging in constructive talk, indeed it is the most common kind of talk they engage in, whilst it is the least likely for their lower achieving counterparts. At the outset of the project, many of the teachers involved felt that talk activities would principally support the writing of lower achievers, and speculated that higher achievers might find the talk activities frustrating and likely to slow down or interrupt the writing process. One feature of the project was pairing children in mixed gender pairs but matched for achievement. This was a research decision enabling comparison of the talk patterns evident in the different achievement pairings. The outcome suggests that children engage in talk opportunities differentially by achievement and this raises pedagogic questions about the efficacy of pairing or grouping children by achievement when engaging in talk activities.

The difference here is not about the volume of talk, but the type of talk produced. High achievers generate more of the talk that is strategically focused on the task, capable of evaluating ideas and written content and that supports and encourages constructive thinking about the task and the text. This implies that it may be better to put together children of different achievement levels or knowledge of English to talk and write as a pair. There is evidence here that would support increased opportunities for classroom talk for its own sake in order to develop talk skills themselves.

What do you think?

> What is the difference between viewing talk as an object of learning or as a means of learning?
> Does talk support writing in the same way for children of differing achievement?

The lessons

The purpose of the talk activities developed by the Talk to Text project was to support writing; the remainder of this chapter looks at how particular talk activities from two lessons impacted on the writing produced. In order to follow this development we will:

- Present lesson outlines drawn from classroom observations to show how the writing activities were used at different points in the lessons to serve different purposes in supporting the children's writing

- Consider a detailed analysis of the classroom talk itself

- Explore a close analysis of some of the writing children produced, looking at it especially in terms of the talk activities that contributed to its production.

Lesson 1: I Can't Ride my Bike

Children observed: Thomas and Sarah whose achievement in writing is about average for the project schools.

This lesson involved retelling a story about a young boy frustrated by his failed attempts to learn to ride his bike. In the role of the young boy the writing task was to write a letter to their father expressing how they felt. For these young writers the particular demands of the task were to write from a perspective other than their own and to focus on the emotive content rather than a chronological series of events. Following the recapping of the story the lesson activities included:

1. Whole class idea generation activities

   - Talk with your partner about how the boy was feeling.
   - The teacher dons a cycle helmet to become the boy in the story and talks to the class in-role about her problem.
   - Talk with your partner about what questions you might ask the boy.
   - The teacher responds in-role to questions from the class.

2. Working with a talk partner at a table

   - Starting 'Dear Dad' talk with your partner about what the letter should include.
   - Tell your partner your opening sentence (oral rehearsal).
   - Magic pencil your opening sentence (oral rehearsal).

Magic pencil: This was an oral rehearsal strategy in which children wrote with their finger saying the sentence as they wrote it, thus the focus was on what they wanted to write and how they were going to write it, not on the secretarial skills required. Talk here is used to shape the written sentence which is very different from the talk that generates ideas. In this classroom the teacher had a strategy printed out and put up on the wall suggesting children might:

THINK IT – SAY IT – MAGIC-PENCIL IT

This approach breaks down the writing process into more manageable cognitive tasks each supported by focused talk activities. Tasks that focused first on ideas, then on ideas framed by sentences spoken aloud, then by rehearsing the act of writing the sentence. The lesson continued with children encouraged to say and magic-pencil each sentence before writing them. The teacher supported the children during writing by encouraging a talk-based approach with their partner either to develop content by generating ideas or to shape sentences through oral rehearsal. This was informed by an intention to habituate the strategic use of talk into the writing behaviour of the children as a means of developing independence in managing the writing process. The teacher paused the writing from time to time to hear children read out some of their sentences, which in turn fed the generation of ideas, and so the strategies should be viewed as iterative rather than sequential.

Lesson 2: The Giant Postman
(from the story by Sally Grindley and Wendy Smith)
Children observed: Tim and Alice – a pair of high achievers.

   The giant postman is so big he frightens the villagers on his round and destroys their gardens. Billy decides to take a letter to the giant, explaining how the villagers feel. The writing task is to continue the story. Following the reading of the story and stopping at a strategic point the lesson activities included:

1. Whole-class idea generation activities

   - Whole-class interactive session about the features of the text displayed on a whiteboard.
   - With your talk partner discuss the situation.
   - Teacher speculates about the content of the letter.
   - Discuss with your partner what needs to go in the letter.
   - Structured paired talk using prompt questions.

     o When did Billy go to the giant's house?
     o How was Billy feeling?
     o What problem did he find when he got there?

2. Working with a talk partner at a table

   - Using the prompt questions say each sentence to your partner before you write it down (oral rehearsal).
   - Talk with your partner about the sentences you have rehearsed (evaluation).

The two lessons both make use of strategies for idea generation and oral rehearsal, thus supporting the children both in the production of content for writing and in the framing of this content into written forms. However the second lesson prioritised child-to-child talk while the first made use of teacher-to-child talk in addition to child-to-child talk. The analysis of the texts produced in each lesson will illustrate how this impacts on writing. There are some interesting issues here, however, about the role of the teacher as guide and model and the extent to which the teacher modelling constrains or supports idea generation. In the first lesson the children were highly engaged in the role play and enjoyed asking their teacher questions, in itself a reversal of the normal pattern of classroom interaction. The teacher was also able to show how a writer might focus on the emotive elements of the story in terms of the boy's frustration rather than just on the events that occurred. The questions and comments the children generated illustrate that in line with their teacher's intentions they were framing the encounter in terms of the boy's feelings. An emphasis that is also evident in the text produced:

> Are you feeling frustrated?
>
> Are you going to give up?
>
> You can do it if you practice some more

The talk activities enabled the children to talk and write from a viewpoint other than their own and to express feelings of frustration – generally expressed verbally – in a written form. This use of teacher modelling, however, also tended to frame all the talk activities that followed. Observing the child-to-child talk when working in pairs reveals how the teacher modelling is reproduced quite closely in their own talk.

In the second lesson, the emphasis was on child-to-child talk and again the impact of this will be seen in the written text. Most of the child-to-child talk took place in the whole-class episodes, this talk was energized and although the children were talking in pairs the classroom observation reveals them overlapping with the conversations of other pairs. Ideas generated through this talk included:

- Telling the giant not to frighten the cat and if he did to get it down from the roof
- To make the giant tidy up his mess in the gardens
- Telling the giant to whisper and tread carefully

Once working at tables, however, the talk and the writing became heavily cued by the prompt questions and remarkably few of the ideas generated through whole-class talk made their way into the final text. A reflection on the use of talk in these lessons might be that in different ways the teachers both create productive and engaging talk opportunities for the children while still exercising a dominant presence in the classroom and therefore, as will be seen, on the writing produced. A recurring theme discussed amongst the project teachers was the struggle to hand over the floor to the children through talk, thus allowing the children agency in determining the nature and direction of the talk while still holding on to their pedagogic control regarding the intended learning objectives.

How do teacher-to-child talk activities differ from child-to-child talk activities? When does teacher support become teacher constraint? Does increasing opportunities for children to talk impact on the power differential in the classroom and should it?

As experts in their own classroom, however, these teachers were aware that talk doesn't just happen and the assumption that talk comes easily to all children is perhaps misplaced. The fact that these teachers felt they needed to support the talk activity itself is a theme returned to later in this chapter.

Talk patterns in the focus lessons

Comparing the two focus lessons reveals a similar pattern of talk to that of the other lessons, with an emphasis on strategic talk, however these two lessons produce disproportionately more strategic talk than is the case for the whole sample and less constructive talk given that the children in The Giant Postman lesson were high achievers.

Table 5.2   Talk patterns in the focus lessons

	Strategic	Evaluative	Constructive
Lesson 1 I Can't Ride my Bike	68%	14%	18%
Lesson 2 The Giant Postman	84%	8%	18%

In both cases this strategic talk is predominantly aimed at text production, through the trying out of sentences using oral rehearsal, and a large amount of this talk is focused on the secretarial aspects of writing. The focus on oral rehearsal is not surprising as both teachers had planned the writing task to focus on this strategic use of talk. There is, however, more evaluative and constructive talk in Lesson One. The children in Lesson One are average achievers, and in

Lesson Two they are high achievers and so the difference between the two lessons is perhaps all the more striking. A possible explanation for these differences may lie with how talk during writing is handled. In The Giant Postman lesson almost all the talk is quiet oral rehearsal almost entirely in one direction, from Alice to Tim. She posits sentences and together they write them down. There is little co-construction of ideas and little evaluation of the sentences suggested. This is in contrast to examples from the previous chapter in which pairs work together to make up and construct possible sentences. The lesson does include examples of different ideas or constructions from Tim, but these are rarely taken up in the talk and in his own text the sentences appear very much as Alice has framed them. Thus the talk is almost exclusively strategic – oral rehearsal to generate text and almost exclusively generated by one of the pair in the talk. In contrast while the I Can't Ride my Bike lesson also includes many examples of this kind of talk there is more talk taking place as the children engage in the act of writing. This talk includes examples of both evaluative and constructive talk, in which the children share ideas and comment on them. So for example there is an episode in which the pair consider the various merits of 'frustrated' or 'fed up' as a means of expressing their feelings. Although little is said in terms of why one might work better, they are heard trying them out in the sentence as they write it, as if listening to and evaluating the difference. In the following example the pair have asked for help because they are struggling to come up with ideas and so the teacher encourages them to role play by asking each other questions:

Sarah	I'm fed up.
Thomas	Why?
Sarah	Because I really want to ride my bike, but it's really rubbish now.
Thomas	Why's it rubbish?
Sarah	Because it's just so rubbish because I keep falling off it and then I keep getting hurt. [pause]
Teacher	Now ask him how he's feeling.
Sarah	What's the matter?
Thomas	I'm really fed up. So I threw my bike …
Sarah	Why are you fed up?
Thomas	Because I threw my bike …

Sarah	Do you like it?
Thomas	No I don't.
Sarah	Why don't you like it?
Thomas	[pause – grin] Because it's crap!
Sarah	[laughs] I really like that!

The analysis of the written texts outlined opposite shows how this exchange not only impacts on what is written, but that the talk itself is revealing. The first exchange shows how Sarah readily expresses her ideas, ideas that eventually become part of the written piece, although the ideas become transformed through the writing process. In contrast Thomas struggles to end his sentence about throwing his bike and as each attempt grinds to a halt Sarah throws in another question to help him. The use of questioning, however, results in the use of 'so' being replaced by 'because' and this enters the written piece as a rather incongruous opening sentence. The knowing and perhaps playful use of the word 'crap' by Thomas is enjoyed by Sarah as a bit of a joke and she uses it in her writing. Thomas presumably never intended his throw-away remark to become part of the writing and although it is his idea he chooses not to use it, perhaps saying something about his own sense of appropriacy.

An additional feature of both these two lessons was that in both cases the girls were the more vocal and tended to dominate the talk and in consequence the final texts. While this does represent stereotypical expectations regarding the verbal female, our videos include plenty of examples of vocal boys playing their part in feeding the alternative stereotype of the dominant male. While these provide examples of how the same behaviour can produce gendered interpretations, by and large the gender of the focus children tended to be less significant in influencing talk patterns than achievement.

Talk into writing

One of the benefits of having a detailed record of classroom talk together with the text that was produced is that it is possible to trace the ideas and sentences in the text back through the lesson to see where the ideas originate and how they develop and change. It is also possible to see whether new ideas are generated at the point of writing. The first stage of the analysis of the children's writing was to track each idea to the point in the lesson where it first appears, this could be with the teacher, an idea from the rest of the class, from their partner or it could be their own idea.

Who do the ideas come from?

The teacher (regular font highlighted)

The class (bold and italic)

The partner (underlined)

Own (regular)

Lesson 1: I Can't Ride my Bike

Thomas
Dear Dad

I'm *fed up* with my bike, because I want to throw it across the garden. I keep falling off. I am going to keep trying to ride it. My sister can ride it – my uncle can ride it. I want *you to help me dad*. Love from

Sarah
Dear Dad

I'm really *fed up* about my bike, because I keep on falling off. The other day I fell off and I really hurt myself. I hurt my foot and my toe because I kicked the bike and I did on my toe.   And when I throw it on the fence I hurt my foot really badly, and it still hurts. I am really furious about it, it is really crap. I really think it is the silliest bike I ever had. I just hate it and I am really *frustrated* about my bike. I really want a new one but I don't want the same bike.

Love from

The impact of the teacher modelling is very clear on these two texts, both pieces of work draw heavily on ideas that come from the original role play enacted by the teacher. However, although Thomas's text is almost entirely dependent on the ideas of others, Sarah, who was working and talking in a pair with Thomas, generated many more new ideas of her own, ideas that do not make their way into Thomas's writing. Sarah, on the other hand, does draw on ideas from Thomas even though these ideas don't make their way into his own text. The more Sarah writes the more she moves away from the teacher model, although she may also be becoming more repetitive. A summary of these two children's writing from this lesson shows the boy's writing as coming mainly from the teacher and the girl's as drawing on multiple sources.

Lesson 2: The Giant Postman

Tim

<u>He delivered it the same day</u>. <u>He wrote it in the afternoon</u>. *He was feeling nervous*. <u>The giant couldn't hear him</u> because he was so high up. <u>The giant couldn't reach the letter</u>

Alice

He delivered the letter the same day. He wrote it in the afternoon. *He was feeling a bit nervous*. The giant was so huge he couldn't hear what he was saying and also, when Billy tried to give him the letter he couldn't reach it because he was a lot more taller than Billy.

The absence of ideas from the teacher in these writing examples from this lesson is a direct consequence of how these activities were set up, in that they built almost entirely on child-to-child talk activities. They are however strongly cued by the prompt questions that supported the oral rehearsal activity, they are also very similar. Generating writing in the context of paired writing is maybe likely to produce similar pieces of writing for each child so perhaps the striking difference between the two pieces of writing from Lesson One is more significant than the similarities in this case. If Thomas in Lesson One used a lot of the teacher's ideas then Tim in this lesson seems to draw heavily on the ideas of his partner, in contrast his partner Alice seems to use her own ideas almost exclusively. What is clear from these examples is that classroom talk does support those who may be highly dependent on the ideas of others for writing content, whether this is the teacher or fellow students.

The second part of the analysis was concerned with how spoken ideas became written text: in some cases the spoken words are written down verbatim, elsewhere they are transformed and shaped, some talk never gets written down and some ideas don't appear until the point of writing.

What do they do with the ideas?

Direct quote – using talk verbatim (*Underlined and italic*)

Transform the ideas – reshaping an idea through writing (**Bold**)

Generate new ideas – ideas that do not appear in the talk activities (*Italic*)

[Unused talk] – individual talk from the focus children that does not appear in the text [Regular – bracketed and highlighted]

Lesson 1: I Can't Ride my Bike

Thomas
Dear Dad

I'm fed up with my bike, **because I want to throw it across the garden**. *I keep falling off. I am going to keep trying to ride it. My sister can ride it – my uncle can ride it*. **I want you to help me dad**. Love from

[I hate my bike, now get me a new bike].
[Girl: why don't you like it *(your bike)*. Boy: Because it's crap]

Sarah
Dear Dad

I'm really fed up about my bike, because I keep on falling off. The other day [when I was at work] *I fell off and I really hurt myself. I hurt my foot and my toe because I kicked the bike and I did on my toe. And when I throw it on the fence* [I nearly threw it across the fence but I didn't] *I hurt my foot really badly and it still hurts. I am really furious about it, it is really crap.*

   I really think it is the *silliest bike* I ever had. **I just hate it and I am really frustrated about my bike. I really want** [I wish I had] **a new one** *but I don't want the same bike.*

Love from

Not only does Thomas draw heavily on the teacher modelling but much of it makes its way verbatim into his writing. The literary form 'my sister can ride it – my uncle can ride it' has been remembered and used just as it was used in the role play. As a piece of text it may be the most literary use of language in any of the writing examples; that the boy remembered it and chose to use it may be as significant as any ideas that he generated himself. In contrast the girl's writing shows that even when she is using ideas that originate with others she frequently transforms and edits these ideas into her own words.

Lesson 2: The Giant Postman

Tim

He delivered it the same day [that he wrote it.] *He wrote it in the afternoon. He was feeling nervous*. [A bit confident but a bit scared.] *The giant couldn't hear him because he was so high up*. [because the boy was so low down]. **The giant couldn't reach the letter.**

Alice

He delivered the letter the same day. *He wrote it in the afternoon. He was feeling a bit nervous* [and a bit worried.] *The giant was so huge* **he couldn't hear what he was saying** *and also, when Billy tried to give him the letter he couldn't reach it because he was a lot more taller than Billy*

While much of this writing is generated by Alice and then written by both of them, Alice occasionally continues to transform the text as she writes it. In contrast Tim tends to use Alice's suggestions although he speaks many ideas that he never writes.

   What is evident here is that children draw on classroom talk for ideas for writing; indeed some children regularly use the ideas of others. This dependence is not necessarily predictive of weak writing, indeed the conscious inclusion of a literary form in the I Can't Ride my Bike example is arguably about the ability to hear what might make good writing. These ideas do not always appear verbatim in written texts but are shaped through talk and some ideas are still being transformed at the point of writing. The prioritising of this shaping and choosing, phrasing and rephrasing through explicit opportunities for evaluation and shared text construction may go some way to refocusing the attention of young writers from the surface features of the writing task to content.

Summary of points for the class teacher

➤ Remember the value of shared writing tasks:

- The need to talk about content
- The possibility of talk about linguistic features
- The need to make choices emphasising writing as design
- The opportunity to hear a variety of possible sentence forms before writing it down.

➤ Share the cognitive demands of scribing

- The value of talk activities during writing as well as before writing
- Oral rehearsal
- Evaluation of word choice and phrasing
- Increasing opportunities for evaluative and constructive talk
- Encouraging text revision during writing.

➤ Experiment with mixed achievement groupings
➤ Remember the value of talk activities for their own sake.

Suggested further reading

Fisher, R. and Larkin, S. (2008) 'Pedagogy or Ideological Struggle? An Examination of Pupils' and Teachers' Expectations for Talk in the Classroom', *Language and Education*, 22(1): 1–16.

Hardman F., Mroz, M. and Smith, F. (2000) 'The Discourse of the Literacy Hour', *Cambridge Journal of Education*, 30(3): 379–90.

Mercer, N. (2000) *Words and Minds: How We Use Language to Think Together*. London: Routledge.

Mercer, N. and Littleton, K. (2007) *Dialogue and the Development of Children's Thinking: a Sociocultural Approach.* London: Routledge.

Mercer, N., Wegerif, R. and Dawes, L. (1999) 'Children's Talk and the Development of Reasoning in the Classroom', *British Educational Research Journal*, 25(1): 95–111.

Myhill, D., Jones, S. and Hopper, R. (2005) *Talking, Listening and Learning: Effective Talk in the Primary Classroom.* Maidenhead: Open University Press.

Lesson plans for write aloud

'Write Aloud' Activity – Invisible Writing

Purpose: To rehearse the words used in a sentence before writing it.

Summary: Children are given a blank sheet of paper and told that there is invisible writing on it. They then 'write over' the invisible writing.

Resources/preparation:

- A familiar text with a strong character with a dilemma/problem/need.
- Blank paper, small whiteboards.

Activity

- Class receives a letter/invitation/diary entry from a known book character, but the page is blank.
- The teacher tells the class the text is written in 'invisible writing'.
- The teacher 'reads' the letter to the class, perhaps using the 'magic finger' technique.
- The teacher gives out a letter (a blank piece of paper) to each child. In talk partners the children are encouraged to talk about what their letter might say.
- The children then go to their tables with their 'letter' and read it to themselves and to their talk partner. They then write over the invisible writing in pencil.

The important thing to emphasise is that only the individual child can read the writing on *their* sheet. It is up to them to say what is written. It is not about guessing what is written or working very hard to see what the character has written. In other words the writing is under complete control of the writer.

Class-based example

A class of Year 1 children have been working on *We're Going on a Bear Hunt* by Michael Rosen. They have read the book, acted out the story using freeze-frames and created music for the journey to the bear's cave.

The teacher has planned a week of literacy work on letter writing and wants to use the book as a vehicle for this work. On the last page of the book is a picture of the bear making his way back to his cave. In the picture he looks very sad and alone. The teacher says she has received a letter from the bear that she wants to share with the class. The letter is a blank sheet. The teacher explains the bear has invisible writing, but she is able to read it. Using the magic finger technique the teacher traces over the invisible writing as she reads the letter to the class. She then writes over the imaginary writing in pencil.

The teacher explains that the children are going to write letters back to the bear. The teacher gives out a blank sheet of paper to each child and says that each piece of paper already has invisible writing on it. The children work in 'write aloud' partners and 'read' their letters to each other. They then move to independent work rehearsing and writing over their invisible writing in pencil.

If this is the first time you have tried this activity …

- This idea may seem a little crazy, but children are happy to engage in this kind of 'make believe'.
- Provide plenty of modelling before sending children to work in pairs and independently.

Teachers who use this activity successfully say things like:

'You can only read the invisible writing on your own letter'
'Let's turn our talking into writing'
'I'm going to trace over the invisible writing with my finger'

'Write Aloud' Activity – Magic Pencil

Purpose: To encourage children to think about writing while they are rehearsing text orally.
Summary: As part of any writing activity, children rehearse their writing by using a magic pencil (or magic finger). This lets them practise what they are going to write before anyone else can see it.
Resources/preparation: • Blank paper • Small whiteboards

Activity

- This is a 'short burst' activity that helps children prepare for writing.
- At the point in a shared session where children are beginning to rehearse what they will write independently, the teacher asks children to rehearse a sentence and write it at the same time with a 'magic finger' or 'magic pencil'.
- The children can write in the air, onto a blank piece of paper, onto a small whiteboard or onto their hand. They can use either an imaginary pencil or their finger.
- This activity can also take place in pairs. Children share their rehearsed sentence and magic finger writing with their partner.
- This activity is useful in fiction and non-fiction writing and across the curriculum.

Class-based example

A class of Year 1 children have been working on the story of *Little Red Riding Hood* with their teacher Sean. They have read the book, acted out the story using freeze-frames and hot-seated the main characters.

The wolf has now gone missing and today the children are writing a 'wanted poster' for Little Red Riding Hood to put up on the trees in the wood. The class looks at a picture of the wolf and in talking partners make up sentences to describe the wolf. The teacher then models what his first sentence will be. He then models saying the sentence and writing it using a 'magic pencil'.

The teacher then shows the children the wanted poster they will be filling in. In talking partners they think of the first sentence they are going to write on their poster. They rehearse it orally with their talk partner. They then rehearse their sentence and write it with their 'magic pencil' on a small whiteboard. The children carry the whiteboards to their tables and begin writing on their wanted posters.

If this is the first time you have done this activity ...

- Make links to the 'sky-writing' children often use when they are learning handwriting.
- Practise all writing the same sentence using a 'magic finger'

Teachers who use this activity successfully might say:

'Say the words as you are writing them!'

'Which were the tricky bits when you were writing with your magic finger?'

'When you get to your table, practise your magic finger writing before you use your pencil'

'Keep your ideas in your head as you walk to your table.'

'Write Aloud' Activity – Paired Writing

Purpose: To rehearse the words used in a sentence before writing it.
Summary: This strategy can be used as part of any writing activity. The children work with 'write aloud' partners. They tell their partner what they are going to write prior to writing.
Resources/preparation: Children arranged in 'write aloud' partners.

Activity

- This is a 'short burst' activity that helps children prepare for writing.
- The teacher organises the class into pairs who can support each other's learning. The pairs are called 'write aloud' partners.
- As they are preparing for writing, the 'write aloud' partners rehearse a small section of their work. This could be a sentence to fill in a speech bubble, the first line of a set of instructions, the opening sentence of their story.
- It is important to keep the tasks for 'write aloud' partners very short and focused – no more than one minute each time.
- The closer the sentence rehearsal to the point of writing the better. It often helps to re-rehearse the sentence in 'write aloud' partners immediately before writing.

Class-based example

A Year 3 class have been working with their teacher Jan on a Design and Technology project to make healthy sandwiches. During the week they have designed, made, and tasted their sandwiches. While they were making their sandwiches the teaching assistant took photos on a digital camera. During the week the children have also read instructions from a variety of books and practised following instructions.

Today's task is to write instructions so that someone else can make their healthy sandwich. Each child comes to the carpet with three digital photos of them making their sandwich. The teacher refers to the poster 'Things to remember when you are writing instructions' they made earlier in the week. She then asks the children to find the first photo in their sequence and share it with their 'write aloud' partner. The 'write aloud' partners then rehearse the first sentence of their sandwich-making instructions. The teacher asks some pairs to share their sentences and then refers again to the poster. Before moving to their tables to begin writing their instructions the 'write aloud' partners rehearse their first sentence one last time.

If this is the first time you have tried this activity …

- Make the children aware that you see talk as work, and that talk supports thinking.
- Set up your 'write aloud' pairs carefully. Will you pair by ability. Will you pair by ability, or use mixed ability pairs?
- How can you best use any classroom help to support children as they work in 'write aloud' partners?
- Set very short tasks for children to complete with their 'write aloud' partners so that they remain on task.

Teachers who use this activity successfully say things like:

'You have 30 seconds to discuss this with your partner.'

'Practise your sentence with your partner.'

'Everyone can share an idea because you've already talked about it with your partner.'

'How did your "write aloud" partner help you with this?'

'Write Aloud' Activity – Talking to a Toy

Purpose: To rehearse the words used in a sentence before writing it.
Summary: This strategy can be used as part of any writing activity. The children work with a toy. They tell their toy what they are going to write, prior to writing.
Resources/preparation: A toy for each child.

Activity

- During shared work the teacher models rehearsing sentences to a toy.
- Each child has a toy as a 'write aloud' partner.
- They practise rehearsing sentences to their toy.
- Children then move to their tables to begin independent writing. They rehearse each sentence with their toy before writing.

Class-based example

A Year 2 class have been on a school trip to a farm. They are now writing a recount of their visit. Their toy animals weren't able to go to the farm with them in case they got dirty, so they will be telling the toys about their trip!

On the interactive whiteboard the teacher has four digital pictures of the visit, but they are in the wrong order. The children and teacher think about the trip and put the pictures in the right order. The teacher models the use of connectives 'first, next, then, at the end'. The children tell the story of their visit to their toys using the connectives and the digital pictures as a stimulus.

At their tables children begin to write independently. They rehearse each sentence to their toy before writing.

Alternative activity

This activity can also work well the other way round. The teacher pretends the toys have been on a visit without the children. The toys whisper their sentences to the children who write them down for them.

If this is the first time you have tried this activity . . .

- Use a toy during shared work and model telling the toy what you are going to write before writing.
- Be very careful about getting children to bring favourite toys into school from home. Loss of a loved toy can involve a lot of time organising a search and much heartache for the child and family!

Teachers who use this activity successfully might say:

'Whisper what you are going to write to your toy.'
'Did your toy understand? Do you need to make any changes to your sentence?'
'Sometimes your toy needs to hear your sentence a few times before they understand it!'

6 Talk For Reflecting On Writing

Shirley Larkin

Introduction

This chapter is about the third of our strategic elements of talk for writing: talk for reflecting on writing. This is what we called 'thinking about writing' for the children but is an aspect of talk for writing that is rather more complex than this simplistic description. It involves two elements: reflection on the process of writing and reflection on the product of writing. In the latter element a child might say or think 'This is a good piece of writing because it is neat'. In the former the child might say or think 'The ending was difficult because I didn't know what to write next and then I remembered my *Red Riding Hood* story.'

So, when we referred to reflection during the Talk to Text project we had to make clear the distinction between these two separate but connected processes of reflection. Reflection on writing referred to children and teachers thinking about and discussing the written script. We found that both teachers and children frequently commented on the secretarial aspects of writing, such as keeping words on the line, writing neatly and using finger spaces. There was also a good deal of reflective discussion about spelling and punctuation. Helping each other with spelling was a common occurrence during the collaborative writing tasks. Some talk partners also engaged in reflection about the content of the writing. This was both in terms of ideas for the writing and suggestions for particular words or images at sentence level. All of these instances of reflection had the writing itself as their object of focus. However, there was another process of reflection which we were interested in facilitating through the project. This is often termed metacognition and it refers to reflection where the object of that reflection is another thought process. Being able to reflect on our own thinking is known to be important for academic success across subject areas. This chapter explores the different features of metacognition and reflection observed during the Talk to Text project. It is important to begin with some understanding of what we mean by metacognition.

Metacognition

Theoretical models of metacognition usually include three distinct features: metacognitive knowledge; monitoring; and control. 'Metacognitive knowledge' includes the knowledge we have about ourselves as learners in relation to a subject area (writing); knowledge we have about particular writing tasks and the context within which we will be working: and knowledge about the kinds of strategies which might help us to reach our goal. It might be something like, 'I know I am quite good at spelling, but not so good at getting good words' or 'I can't concentrate on writing when it is noisy'. All of this metacognitive knowledge we build up over time and with experience through engaging with many different writing tasks, in different situations. Receiving feedback about our achievement on different tasks also helps us to build a metacognitive knowledge base. Not all of the metacognitive knowledge we build up over time will be reliable and accurate. We might believe ourselves to be poor writers because of one particular task or instance of negative feedback and this has obvious connotations for our future motivation to engage with new writing tasks. Bringing our knowledge about ourselves as writers to conscious awareness can help us to overcome these negative beliefs.

This sort of metacognitive knowledge can be useful in enabling us to make connections between a new writing task and something we have attempted before. Drawing on this aspect of metacognitive knowledge makes us question whether or not we understand what is required in the task, whether or not we have all the information we need or how we can best use our existing resources to meet the task demands.

Metacognitive knowledge about strategies refers not to the strategies we might use for spelling difficult words or mnemonics for factual information, but to our knowledge of strategies for reaching our writing goal. These might include knowing that taking the time to plan a piece of writing will pay off in the end or that it is necessary to stop and reflect on our writing as we go along. The ability to use appropriate metacognitive strategies during a task is often referred to as metacognitive skill. We will see examples of the children in the Talk to Text project drawing on their metacognitive knowledge and demonstrating metacognitive skills later in the chapter.

The other two factors of metacognition are interconnected. These are usually referred to as 'monitoring' and 'control'. Research tells us that learners who monitor their own thinking during a task tend to be motivated and self-reliant learners who achieve well in academic subjects. Skilled writers have been shown to move between reflecting on how they are thinking about the writing task and producing the writing. We described this process more fully in Chapter 1. These movements may be brief and fleeting pauses, or much longer periods of reflection. Monitoring our own thinking requires us to pause and shift our attention from the task itself to focus on how we are thinking about the task. By doing this we are able to make conscious decisions about how to progress and to evaluate how close we are to achieving our goal.

During the Talk to Text project we worked with the teachers to encourage the children to reflect in this metacognitive way as well as to reflect on the writing itself. This was perhaps one of the more difficult aspects of the project to achieve. Metacognition, if it is encouraged at all, tends to be viewed as something to focus on with much older children. The kind of reflection common in primary class-rooms through three-part lesson structures has tended to be an evaluation in the concluding or plenary session of how difficult or easy the task has been or what kinds of things have been learned through the session. In Talk to Text we were asking teachers to think differently about reflection, to consider how they might encourage these much younger children to think about their own thinking during a task and not just in a final plenary session.

It is difficult for adults, let alone for children, to reflect on their own thinking after an event. To do so would require a good deal of conscious awareness and a reliable memory. It is fair to say that encouraging metacognition in the younger children on the project was a challenge for all the teachers and for us in creating writing tasks which would require this type of reflection. You can read in the following 'Interlude' one teacher's thoughts on this.

Tasks for encouraging reflection

In working with the teachers to create writing tasks for the project we aimed to provide opportunities for children to reflect on both their writing and their thinking throughout each task. However, some tasks were specifically created to encourage metacognition. Amongst these we suggested the idea of a 'thinking cap' where children in pairs would take it in turns to put on an actual cap and then reflect on and talk about a piece of their own writing with their talk partners. You can find an example of a lesson using this technique in the section of lessons using talk for reflection: 'Thinking Cap' (p. 148). They might think about the aim of the writing and what they were trying to achieve in the piece as well as reflecting on the process of producing the writing, so asking themselves questions such as 'Where did I get my ideas from?' 'What did I do when I got stuck?' 'What was I thinking about when I was writing this?' 'What was I feeling when I wrote this?' 'Could I have done it differently?' They might also evaluate the writing in terms of their own goals and begin to develop self-assessment skills.

Another activity concentrated much more on the evaluative aspect by suggesting that the children use a checklist of criteria to evaluate a piece of published writing. These criteria included thinking about the type of writing, and the author; comparing the text to others they already know; and also reflecting on how the writing makes them feel. In order to develop metacognition about self as a writer it is necessary to make explicit what writers are and what they do. An example of a lesson like this can be found in the section of lessons using talk for reflection: 'Two Ticks and a Wish'. (p. 150)

The 'Self as Writer' task encouraged the children to think about themselves as writers. They were asked to imagine themselves as a famous writer and then write about the kinds of books they write and for what audience. They also thought about how they get their ideas for their books, what they do when they get stuck and what others such as critics and reviewers say about their books. This activity could obviously lead on to producing books in the classroom. World Book Day during the project year provided a focus for this activity.

In order to develop metacognition, theory tells us that we need to have metacognitive experiences, that is, we need to come across situations where our thinking is challenged; where there may be more than one approach that can be taken; where the decisions we make are important; and where we need to plan and evaluate. Writing tasks which will provide these types of experiences need to be multi-faceted and substantial. We do not need to engage in much reflection in order to make a simple list, but if we are asked to produce a list of tips for writing for a particular audience we need to consider the needs of that audience and how best to organise and structure the information as well as what information we need to include. One task in this set of reflection tasks focused particularly on being able to take on another perspective. This task involved the children in producing a guide to help other children either write a story or write an information text. This task is also described in the chapter on idea generation (Chapter 3).

In order to do this task well the children needed to be able to put themselves in the place of the readers of the text. In this case the readers of the text would be a year younger, so the project children had to reflect on what they knew and were able to do when they were a year younger. This made for some interesting speculation between talk partners. In one session after the children had provided a list of tips for writing instructions the whole class reflected on how useful their instructions would be and how easy or difficult they had found the exercise. One child realised that younger children may not know what she knows:

Child   They might not know what command words are.

Teacher   They might not, so who could tell them what command words are?

Child 2   Us.

Teacher   Us, yes they could come and ask us. What else could help them if they didn't know?

Child 3   They could ask their teacher.

The first child has clearly made a metacognitive shift from thinking about the content or organisation of the instruction list to thinking about how effective the list will be for its target audience. The other children also demonstrate some limited strategies for gaining knowledge. This is a beginning of reflection on self as a writer and could be extended through further questioning by the teacher or lead into a follow-up task about strategies for finding information. Only through repeated exposure to types of tasks where there is a *need* to shift perspective, will children develop the skills to do this for themselves.

What other questions could the teacher have asked?

Developing language for reflection

One of the reasons that metacognition has been seen as developing in later childhood is because younger children often do not use what are termed mental state words, with consistency. Mental state words allow us to communicate about our own thinking. They include words such as: 'think', 'guess', 'believe', 'imagine', 'know'. As we mature and experience these words in different contexts we come to a common understanding of what we mean by them. This is obviously useful, but it can also become an automated and habitual use of language, which does not accurately describe what we mean. We may say 'know' when we are really referring to a belief or we may not distinguish between 'believe' and 'understand', for example 'She said it was true, but I don't understand it'. We probably do understand that the other person is making a claim that something is true, we may even understand the basis of this claim, but we are using understand to mean that we do not share this position. Our automatic use of these words can be confusing for children who have yet to develop their own understanding of these words. Studies of language development have shown that understanding of these words develops during the early years, but 6- and 7-year-old children may still use these mental state words inconsistently.

Research on children's non-verbal imaginative play suggests that even very young children are able to reflect and see things from another's point of view prior to the development of their use of these mental state words. This means that it is important for adults to encourage reflection and metacognition in young children regardless of their perceived language ability. There is a reciprocal relationship between developing understanding of mental state words and developing metacognition. By teachers introducing and modelling these words children not only develop the ability to communicate their thinking, but also develop their ability to reflect on their thinking.

It is not uncommon for children to pick up the habit of starting their verbal responses to teachers' questions designed to get them to reflect on their thinking, with the simple phrases 'I think' or 'I thought about it in my head'. These phrases may be indicators of metacognition, but not necessarily so. It depends very much on what comes next and on the context in which the phrase is uttered. Two examples from the Talk to Text project below will indicate the difference. In response to a teacher's question about what had helped the children to complete a writing task one child answered:

I thought about it in my head.

A second child answered:

I remembered writing instructions before and I knew how to do this one.

Initially, the first answer may appear to be more metacognitive because it refers directly to thinking and to some view about where thinking is located. Young children often learn this kind of phrase in order to respond to any questions about reflection. The problem is that it is difficult to know whether the first child is actually reflecting on thought processes or simply repeating a phrase she's heard before.

In the second example the child is clearly reflecting as he draws a comparison between the present task and a previous task. He also uses two mental state words, 'remembered' and 'knew'. His response makes sense because he is using those two words differently.

When faced with responses similar to those by the first child we would encourage the child to elaborate on the idea of thinking and try to re-capture one of the thoughts which had helped them to do the task. However, having said this, it is not a good idea to press children for more information about their own thinking if they are clearly struggling to articulate this. Instead teachers can model the use of these mental state words throughout a task by referring to their own thinking. It is sometimes necessary with young children to make the distinctions between the words explicit, as in 'Why did I use the word "guess" there?' or 'Does he know where the treasure is hidden or is he guessing?' 'How do you know that?', etc. These are all things that good teachers do, but sometimes without being conscious of why. As teachers, reflecting on your own use of language can initiate new ways to support the development of children's language for reflection.

Do you model 'thinking words'?
Are there any opportunities within your lessons to help children develop this language?

Developing metacognition together

As with other aspects of development, children will develop their metacognitive knowledge and skills at different rates. In any classroom there will be a range of low to high metacognitive skill but these levels are not necessarily linked to high achievement in a particular subject area, or to high levels of verbal ability. However, social interaction and especially talk is important for developing higher levels of reflection. It is through sharing and explaining our ideas that we bring our own thinking to conscious awareness. Through shared talk we also construct new ideas and thoughts. In order to develop metacognitive skills we need to practise reflecting on those ideas and listening to the comments of others as well as simply expressing our views. This is a difficult skill to learn and it takes time, support and opportunity. Through the talk partners on the project the teachers encouraged children to reflect on their ideas, to slow down the process of writing, to plan properly and to consider different options for the task.

The talk partners were, as far as possible, of equivalent achievement level in terms of literacy and were boy/girl pairs in each case. The pairs remained constant throughout the project and this meant that children got to know their talk partner well and began to develop a working relationship with them. Whilst achievement level played some part in the production of the written texts, the ability to discuss and reflect both on thinking and writing was not so clearly determined by academic achievement. It was clear that there was a good deal of individual difference in terms of reflection, both between and within pairs.

When we analysed the videos for examples of metacognition and reflection we developed a number of categories of different kinds of reflection. These were divided between children's demonstrations of reflection and metacognition and what teachers did to support and facilitate this (see Table 6.1).

Table 6.1 Child and teacher codes for reflection

Child codes (C=child)	Teacher codes (T=teacher)
C asks C what they think	T asks for checking
C error correction	T asks for evaluation of difficulty
C monitors thinking	T asks for task comprehension
C NVC error correction	T asks how do you know
C planning	T facilitates self knowledge about writing
C refers to classroom environment	T non-verbal communication about thinking
C refers to joint knowledge	T missed opportunity for metacognition
C refers to own thinking	T models a strategy for spelling

Table 6.1   (Continued)

Child codes (C=child)	Teacher codes (T=teacher)
C refers to self as writer	T models planning strategy
C refers to talk as a strategy	T refers to how decision is reached
C refers to task strategy	T refers to past knowledge
C shows that they can take another perspective	T refers to remembering
C to C constructing ideas	T refers to taking another perspective
C to C planning	T refers to talking with partners
	T refers to thinking about writing
	T sets up collaboration

In this section I will concentrate on children's metacognition and reflection on writing, picking out some examples from the data to expand on the categories in Table 6.1. One of the most frequent examples of children monitoring their joint work was the spotting and correction of errors. This is a low level of metacognition but one which is important not only for the production of text, but also for developing awareness of self as a writer. Error correction involves us in evaluating and monitoring writing. Through this we become more aware of the different levels at which writing works and eventually of how to plan our writing to meet a specific objective. This evaluative aspect is clear in the talk of these two writing partners as they reflect on the phrases they are creating to describe the sensory experience of riding a bicycle down a steep hill.

The girl in this partnership is writing a phrase on a strip of paper whilst the boy watches closely over her shoulder:

Boy   Oh no you've done it wrong. I can see whizzing harshly doesn't make sense does it?

Girl   [Stops writing and reads her phrase]

Boy   Whizzing harshly past my face doesn't make sense does it?

Girl   [Shakes her head]

Boy   Let's do it again. [He takes the paper and screws it up.]

In this partnership whilst the girl came up with some creative ideas for phrases, the boy was often monitoring and evaluating to make sure that the ideas made sense both grammatically and in terms of the task.

In this second excerpt he again comments on the sense of the phrase.

Girl   I can hear the wind flying

Boy   Whistling past [pause] no

Girl   Flying. That's the good one.

Boy   You can't hear flying. I can hear the wind

Girl   rustling past

Boy   no, rustling in the trees

Girl   rustling in the trees [nods]

Boy   no, rustling the leaves

Girl   yeah, rustling the leaves.

Here the boy is not only correcting errors but continues to evaluate the ideas after the error has been corrected. He is both self monitoring and taking on the role of group monitor for his writing partnership. Later in this writing session the boy comes up with a strategy for writing the rest of the phrases:

Boy   Shall we do a 'see' next and then a 'hear'?

Girl   Yeah

Boy   OK just write 'I can see' first and then we can talk about it.

They go on to complete the task in this way, splitting the phrases up into three different stages: firstly deciding on which one of the five senses they will focus on; then deciding on the noun (e.g. the wind, the air, the trees, etc.); and finally deciding on the best verb and sometimes adverb to use. They did not, of course, use these actual terms in their talk but they had clearly organised themselves to complete the task in this way. In order to come up with this strategy the boy has had to reflect on the process of writing the phrases, not just on the content. He is keeping in mind the final objective of the task to produce a variety of phrases to capture different sensory experiences of riding a bicycle. In this way the boy is monitoring the partnership's progress towards their goal. The strategy he proposes is aimed at completing the task and has arisen out of his reflection on the task, himself and strategies he is aware of. It may also be that he is reflecting on the skills of his writing partnership, although we cannot be sure of this.

   It may appear from these excerpts that the girl is playing a more passive role in this talk partnership, but video footage shows that she is fully involved and the boy continuously seeks her approval before moving on. He also refers back to her to help keep the task on track and to check that they are still meeting the task objectives.

She often responds non-verbally and this is an important feature of young children's socially constructed metacognition which sometimes get lost in the focus on analysing talk. Non-verbal metacognition is also often demonstrated by children who do not have English as their first language, who have yet to develop the verbal fluency in English to communicate their thinking. The benefit of having video footage of children working together meant that we could also look at non-verbal communication and this came to be an important aspect of observing the variety of ways in which children reflected on the task and on their own thinking.

Other strategies focused on the organisation of the writing partnership to produce a co-constructed text. Whilst some children naturally fell into taking turns to write the next bit of text and others were directed to do so by the teacher, other children spent some time negotiating and deciding on the best way to work together. Allowing children the time to organise themselves in terms of the task demands facilitates collaboration and encourages self regulation. In the same way as in our adult lives, through negotiating collaborative tasks we become aware of our own skills as well as those of our partners.

Planning

Other metacognitive skills which we observed children developing through their talk partners included planning how to begin the task and planning how to present the finished work. In some sessions teachers had children writing on Post-it notes or on strips of paper so that they could concentrate on co-constructing the ideas for writing first before thinking about organising those ideas. Physically moving strips of paper around can be a useful aid to reflecting on how the text might be understood by a reader.

Planning is a complex metacognitive skill, which is dependent upon the ability to reflect. It involves allocation of resources such as time and attention, as well as having an overview of a task, engaging in deliberate control of the task, making decisions and making use of self knowledge. Planning is a sophisticated skill which many adult learners lack. It is particularly difficult for young children. However, given the opportunity, some children in the project began to talk about how they might approach the writing task. In this excerpt two children who are underachieving in writing are involved in a collaborative writing task about animal habitats and behaviour. The teacher has structured the activity so that each child first decides on what animal they will represent, then they take it in turns to ask each other a series of teacher-given questions about that animal and its habits. The writing task involves the children in filling in a grid about different animals, their behaviour and possible threats to their survival. Although the activity has been structured and organised by the teacher, these two children still engage in some planning of how they will manage the task:

The girl appears confused about the grid for writing and instead writes her name on the back of the paper.

Girl   [Watches boy writing in the grid] I don't know how to write it.

Boy   [Pointing to the grid] You can write them in there.

Girl   But you have to draw the animals.

Boy   Yes but we can draw the animals later. You can start with these ones [pointing to the grid] and then go down or you can start here [pointing to the left hand side] and go across. I started from the top.

Girl   Ok I'll do this line then.

Boy   We need to do some.

Girl   OK I'll do this one and this one [pointing to different places on the grid].

They begin to write in silence.

The boy in this partnership has a good idea of the overall task and what the grid should look like when it is complete. By reflecting on this he is able to guide the girl towards a strategy for writing which will not only complete the task, but will allow them to do so collaboratively.

The majority of the writing partnerships did not engage in this type of organisational planning. Instead they tended to jump into writing without considering their joint goal. When the task was fairly simple or when the children were producing individual pieces of writing this was not so much of a problem, but when the task was about producing a collaborative piece of writing the lack of planning about how to organise the task between themselves led to problems. Sometimes it was not made clear by teachers whether children should be producing an individual piece of writing or a collaborative piece and this caused some confusion.

Good planners have been shown to be more flexible and capable of shifting their attention between different elements of a task. Good planners also tend to draw on their past knowledge of similar tasks, are able to keep their goal in mind and keep to their plan as the task progresses. Ineffective planners on the other hand tend to switch between objectives in a more chaotic manner. The non-verbal behaviour of children writing showed that some children found it very difficult to maintain the teacher's plan for their writing throughout the task. They would often switch between generating ideas with their talk partners, focusing on spelling individual words, talking about the task in general, writing their names or date and then using a strategy such as magic pencil. Teachers were seen to give very clear plans for the writing, which meant that there was little necessity for the children to think about how to approach the writing task for themselves. Allowing the children to take control of the task, including planning, allows for the possibility of failure to plan. This is not necessarily a bad thing. Failure to plan, which results in a less effective running of the task, can lead to new metacognitive knowledge. Teachers may draw attention to the effects of failure to plan, and children should be encouraged to think about how well they have planned their work and the impact this has had on the finished product.

Monitoring and control

Self-monitoring and control are two connected but different metacognitive processes. Self-monitoring is viewed as a bottom-up process, which refers to keeping track of where you are in relation to a goal and involves evaluating progress towards that goal. Control is seen as a top-down process which involves adopting new strategies to cope with the task as it progresses.

During the project children were observed monitoring themselves and their partners in terms of progress towards completion of the writing task and in terms of quantity and secretarial quality of the writing produced. For instance, children competed with others on their tables to complete the tasks quickly: 'We're on our last one as well', 'We've put all of ours in order already', 'We've finished'. Whilst this behaviour indicates some awareness of progress on the task, there was little monitoring beyond this level of the quality of the work produced except for in terms of neatness or correct spelling. However, some talk partners did engage in reflection on the strategies they were using to complete the task.

There were some instances of children asking each other about their own work and using the partnership to help them to get started, as in this short exchange:

Boy   You've got to still give me some questions and then we'll start writing.

Girl   Can't think of a question.

Boy   Do you want to start writing our first ones down?

Girl   Don't know what to write.

Boy   You can start with these ones [referring to questions they had already generated] and then go down. I started from the top.

The boy here is taking on the role of group monitor, but the girl is also monitoring her own progress on the task and uses the talk partnership to give her the push necessary to start the writing task. The partnership is acting as a facilitator or permission giver, which enables the girl to move beyond her feeling of having no more ideas, to the next step of producing writing. During the project talk partnerships were often seen to provide this service. The feeling of being stuck at one place in the task can be alleviated through talk with a partner.

The girl in the following talk partnership is reflecting on what the partnership has already achieved in order to justify the strategy they have chosen.

The pair are considering a list of instructions which they have written on individual strips of paper and having organised them and stuck them down they wonder about the one they have left out:

Girl   We already know that number 2 is the least important, so that's why we didn't write it.

Boy   I think so too.

As well as providing a justification for their final piece of writing, the girl is making explicit her own thinking and reflection on their earlier discussion. In this sense she is providing a peer model of reflection. In a Vygotskian sense she has internalised the earlier peer-to-peer talk and is now able to represent it to her partner in a way which is strategic and useful for completion of the task.

Evaluating

Evaluating at task level is a metacognitive skill which relies on the ability to hold in mind the goal of the task and to judge the extent to which the goal has been met. Some talk partnerships did engage in evaluation of the task for themselves. This was most often at a level of having finished the task and having completed all the required steps. Non-verbal responses showed that children were often pleased to have completed the task but there were few child-to-child instances of reflecting on the quality of the work produced. There were more instances of children comparing the quantity of work produced with other groups on their table. Yet evaluating is an important aspect of writing. Skilled writers read and re-read their writing in order to evaluate the extent to which it meets different goals and then go on to use this evaluation to edit and make changes. Evaluation takes place at both word and sentence level as we seek to formulate our ideas and also following the task when we read through and make a judgement about quality and fitness for purpose. The children in the project did engage in some word and sentence level evaluation as shown above, but little self-instigated evaluation of the quality of the completed writing.

Evaluation was most often initiated by the teacher and left to the plenary session at the end of the lesson. However, it was clear that when teachers did ask for evaluation, children were able to evaluate their writing and the strategies they had used to complete it. It was in some of these exchanges that we observed more metacognition.

In this excerpt the teacher of a Year 1 class is trying to get the children to evaluate and identify the difference between talking and writing:

The children are sitting on the carpet just before lunchtime break.

Teacher	Put your hand up if you found the talking the easiest part. [About half put up their hands, although some are obviously hedging and some are clearly not listening to the question.]
Teacher	Eesha why did you find the talking the easiest part?
Eesha	[Answers but noise from within and outside the classroom makes it difficult to hear]
Teacher	Oh did you hear that? I don't think everyone did because they are talking. Eesha said that she found the talking the easiest part because she said that writing the words is harder than talking the words and talking the words is easier than writing the words.

The teacher asks the question the other way round and gets a similar brief answer. It is clear that she is struggling to get any meaningful reflection from the children in this final part of the lesson. This is a common problem with trying to get young children to evaluate their thinking or learning after the task is complete. It is particularly problematic for young children to judge the ease or difficulty of a task because they are unable to compare it with similar tasks or past experience. Only after we have built up a considerable metacognitive knowledge base about ourselves as learners in different context can we really say whether we have found a task easy or difficult. Without this we may make a judgement that we have found the task easy, but then we may not have completed it successfully or we may claim that a task is difficult because we have not engaged in it fully rather than because we know that we have worked really hard to comprehend it and have drawn on all of our resources and knowledge of strategies. Being able to evaluate after a task is something which develops with age and with experience and in this second excerpt a Year 2 teacher is having more luck with engaging the children in this type of reflection after the task.

Teacher	Jane how did you find that writing today, was it easy, hard?
Jane	Easy
Teacher	What made it easy, what did you have today or do today that helped you make that writing easy?
Jane	Because I practised writing it first with my finger.
Teacher	Did anything else help anybody?
Boy 1	The room being quiet
Boy 2	Reading a book first
Girl 1	Thinking
Boy 3	Having lines to write on
Boy 4	Thinking in your head first and then writing it
Girl 2	Magic pencil
Teacher	Anything else before we started writing what did we do, in your pairs
Few children	Talking about it
Teacher	Did talking help you, put up your hands if it did. [Most children put their hands up, but some say no.] Some of you found that talking about it helped you, some of you found that practising the writing first helped you, some of you found that writing with a magic pencil helped you.

What's helped you check your writing in the end, if you have got that far?

Girl 3   The checklist [referring to a list on each table of things to check in writing such as capital letters, full stops, etc.].

In this excerpt the teacher has more luck in getting the children to reflect on what they have done through the lesson partly because the children are older (they are 7), but also because she follows up the first answer of 'easy' with a request for more explanation.

She also continues to ask for examples and summarises these before moving on to the final phase of the lesson which is to re-read the written text and check for punctuation, spelling and other errors using a checklist.

This period of reflection is at the end of the lesson, but it is not the last thing the children do. Instead, by putting one of the strategies into practice immediately the teacher is reinforcing how becoming aware of how we write, what makes writing easy and difficult, is useful in helping us to produce a good piece of work, free of errors. Repeated use of this type of questioning by this teacher was seen to develop children's ability to reflect over the course of the project. The children in her class became increasingly aware of the strategies they were using and of the aspects of writing they were finding difficult, whether this was getting ideas for writing, spelling or joined up writing. See Corinne's own reflection on this in the Interlude following this chapter.

Individual metacognition

Whilst developing metacognition is facilitated through peer collaboration and teacher questioning, the aim is that children become more aware of themselves as writers and begin to ask themselves the same questions. Knowing whether or not you understand the task and knowing about how you write will enable you to choose the best strategies for organising the task. Skilled writers tend to have a sophisticated understanding of what type of writer they are. For instance do I think of the writing as a whole first or do I begin with a section and build up from there? Do I know the end of my story before I begin, or do I allow my writing to be led by the characters? Do I make detailed plans for each section, chapter or paragraph or do I have an overall outline and then write more freely and move sections around later on? I might also come to know things about myself as a writer in terms of the context in which I am writing. So do I prefer to write at certain times of the day and does this depend on what type of writing I am doing? Do I prefer to write with background music, or in silence? Do I set myself writing goals to complete a certain amount in a certain time or do I write as a flow and only stop when I am tired? Experienced writers have different ways of writing which are effective for them.

Children need to be provided with opportunities to think about how they write. The aim is not to build a fixed portrait of 'myself as writer' but to encourage the process of consistent reflection on self as writer, which acknowledges that at different times we might approach writing in different ways and recognises that writers may go about things in different ways.

One way of encouraging this reflection is to encourage children in self questioning. This might begin with children asking themselves if they understand the task and then go on to asking themselves about how they will organise and begin the task. Self questioning often leads to self doubt so children need to be reminded of strategies they can use to help themselves should they become stuck on the writing task. This type of reflection, whilst aided by a group plenary session, is often best not left wholly to the end of the lesson. Through the project we witnessed many examples of teachers visiting group tables and engaging children in reflection through simple questions. In this excerpt the teacher is working with a boy/girl pair of struggling writers who are trying to write some text to accompany a picture of themselves. They have to begin with 'I like to ...'

Teacher to girl	I like to ... what do you like to do at playtime?
Girl	Skipping
Teacher	So I like to ...
Girl	Skipping
Teacher	Do you like to skip or Do you like to skipping?
Girl	Skip
Teacher	So what are you going to write?
Girl	I like to skip.
Teacher	Yes, how do you know that's what you should write?
Girl	Because I said it first.

The teacher then engages the boy in a similar conversation but here the focus is more on spelling out the words than on making the sentence sound right. After sounding out one word the teacher asks 'How do you know what to write?' The boy refers to the board, 'That word is on the board'. The teacher asks 'So what do you need to do?' The boy answers 'I can copy that'. The teacher's questioning here has focused both children's attention on the strategies they can use to work out how to write the next sentence. In this way the teacher is facilitating the children's reflection on their own knowledge of the strategies and not just providing them with strategies. This encourages metacognition and through repeated exposure to these types of questions, children begin to internalise these questions and to ask them of themselves. This is a step towards becoming a self-regulated writer.

Developing metacognition is a slow and gradual process. It needs to be facilitated in different ways throughout the lesson rather than just being left to the plenary session at the end.

The teacher's role

Teachers are vital in fostering metacognition and reflection in young children. This may be done through questioning as seen above, but it is also important that teachers model their own thinking. In order to do this teachers also need to become aware of how they are thinking at a given time. This involves shifting the focus of attention from the task to how we are thinking about the task. In the Talk to Text project we encouraged teachers to engage in self reflection through keeping an audio diary of the different sessions. We asked teachers not only to reflect on their teaching during these sessions but also on their own thoughts about themselves as writers. We also ran a writing workshop session where both the research team and the teachers engaged in some creative writing and some reflection on this process. Through engaging with our own reflections on writing we are better placed both to model how to reflect and also to create new ways of fostering reflection and metacognition in the classroom. The types of questions teachers asked in order to facilitate reflection included the following.

How questions
How do you know that? How did you think of that idea? How did you decide what to write? How did you plan your work? How did you check your work? How could you make your writing even better?

What questions
What did you do when you got stuck? What could you do if you don't know how to spell the word? What types of ideas did you have? What was good about your writing? What would you do differently if you did this writing again? What helped you with your writing?

Why questions
Why did you choose that idea? Why did you write this bit first? Why did you talk to your partner? Why do we need to check our work? Why will other people want to read our writing? Why did you use magic pencil?

As we saw in some of the earlier examples, teachers also asked children to evaluate the ease or difficulty of the writing task. This was not always successful and can be problematic with children not wanting to say that they found writing difficult when it appears that their peers are agreeing that it was an easy task. It is probably more beneficial to ask children what helped them with their writing and how they might improve it, than to concentrate on ease or difficulty. We also need to be careful that we do not get children to be ashamed of difficulty. Finding something difficult and getting over it is a really important experience.

It is important to remember why we are asking these questions in the first place. The focus should be on facilitating the children's ability to reflect on themselves and on their writing. This may mean that you need to model some of this reflection yourself, and provide younger children with some examples of the language we need to talk about our thinking. Creating an environment which is conducive to developing reflective writers requires reflective teachers, who know when to stand back and let children organise and plan their own tasks, and when to step in with some helpful questions or suggestions. Most teachers engage in some of these ways of fostering reflection, but in order to develop reflective and self-regulated writers you need to be conscious of doing this and strategic in developing and sustaining ways of doing this. Through developing the metacognitive awareness of your young writers you are likely to see a development in their attitudes towards writing.

> How might developing reflection impact on learning?
> Can metacognition sometimes be negative or debilitating?
> Is it possible to foster reflective learners within the constraints of the curriculum?

Summary of points for the class teacher

- ➢ Help children to identify the writing goal.
- ➢ Foster a questioning attitude, beginning with 'Do I understand the task?'
- ➢ Help children to make conscious their knowledge of writing strategies.
- ➢ Give children the responsibility for planning the task.
- ➢ Encourage children to ask questions of each other and to share writing strategies.
- ➢ Model the language of thinking and encourage children to be specific about the language they use.
- ➢ Reiterate for children what they are doing when they write, for example planning, organising material, concentrating on spelling, etc.
- ➢ Model your own thinking by 'thinking aloud'.
- ➢ Engage children in discussion about themselves as writers.

Suggested further reading

Fisher, R. (2002) 'Shared Thinking: Metacognitive Modelling in the Literacy Hour', *Reading, Literacy and Language* (now called *Literacy*), 36 (2): 64–8.

Israel, S.E., Collins Block, C., Bauserman, K.L., Kinnucan-Welsch, K. (eds) (2005) *Metacognition in Literacy Learning, Theory, Assessment, Instruction and Professional Development*. Mahwah, NJ: Lawrence Erlbaum.

Larkin, S. (2010) *Metacognition in Young Children*. Abingdon: Routledge.

Interlude 3

The Art of Reflection

Corinne Bishop

Class teacher

I particularly enjoyed developing reflection in my literacy lessons. This is an area where most of my colleagues felt least confident, possibly an area neglected by many teachers, myself included.

At the beginning of the project reflection meant simply asking the children how they felt about their writing, showing their thoughts by a thumbs up, level or down, or by drawing three circles for confident, two for getting there, one for needing more help. The children quickly became adept at this level of self assessment but were not thinking any more deeply about why their writing was easy or difficult.

I then began to ask the children what made their work easy, what had helped them with their work, what made the writing hard? We spent time looking at the strategies I and they had used in the lessons to support their writing, and deciding on the influence those strategies had made upon their writing. The strategies we used and discussed included drama, teacher-in-role, hot-seating characters, teacher modelling writing a sentence or paragraph, partner talk, invisible writing with a 'magic' pencil/feather, telling a sentence to a toy, prompt sheets for writing a sentence, a recount, a postcard, etc., word banks and dictionaries. This kind of questioning and analysis generally took place at the end of a lesson in the plenary.

From there I embarked on whole lessons of reflection where children used their knowledge about writing in a particular genre to make help sheets for another class or year group.

For example, after we had worked on writing a recount the children made prompt sheets for Year 1 children to use for their writing the following week. The children worked in mixed ability pairs. Together the children had to decide which were the most important features of the style of writing they had just completed. Then they wrote their ideas on strips of paper. After completing a series of strips they discussed together which order to put the features in, beginning with the ones they thought were most important. The strips were then stuck down in their agreed order. During the plenary of these lessons we compared different pairs' ideas and discussed the order they had chosen. These activities really made the children think hard about what they had learned to do in their writing, what was important and why.

So, what impact has this made on children's learning? The children have all learned to work better cooperatively, recognising their partner's strengths and weaknesses and providing support for each other. They have become more aware of their own strengths and areas for development. They know what helps them to learn and can find or ask for specific support, becoming more independent learners. Through talk and reflection the children have become far more aware of what they need to do in order to improve their writing.

Talking About Writing – What The Children Told Us

Ros Fisher

Introduction

Tom sits quietly in his chair. His face is blank. He stares seemingly at nothing. Charlotte is beside him. She looks around at what is going on around them. Tom does not seem interested. The class are all moving from sitting on the carpet to their chairs in readiness to start writing. They have been talking about healthy eating and are about to write some notes on keeping healthy. The pencils are in a pot on the desk and a Teaching Assistant is about to give out the paper for them to use. Tom still stares off into the distance. Another child at the table puts his hand down in front or Tom, another places her hand on top, and another, and another. Soon three or four children (all off screen) are playing at piling up their hands one on top of the other. Tom's eyes shift towards the piling hands. Charlotte joins in. And then Tom too joins in. His eyes shining, laughing, animated. The Teaching Assistant comes over with the paper for the children on the table, the hands disappear and Tom's blank look returns.

For the next half hour Tom sits quietly. He says only a few words when working with his talk partner. He holds his pencil and writes when the teacher comes over. He is quiet, docile, with a face that shows little or no evidence of interest, pleasure or even effort or worry. The only change to this is when another child on the table invites him to compare the heights of their pencils. Tom brightens up. He organises the table to see whose pencil is the longest but soon returns to his blank demeanour.

How many children can we think of who are in some way or another like Tom? Identified by his teacher as underachieving in writing, he wrote the minimum that he could get away with but caused no problem to anyone. What can we learn from what children feel about writing that might help motivate them to engage in writing with something like the pleasure and animation that Tom engaged with the simple game of piling up hands?

All teachers know how much it matters to have a class who are engaged with what is happening in the classroom and who understand what they are meant to be learning. Throughout this book we have emphasised the complexity of writing as an activity – it is unsurprising that some children struggle with learning what it is all about.

Socio-cultural theories of learning emphasise the importance of taking into account the learner as well as the curriculum and the teacher. No one who has taught young children can disagree with the fact that there is 'many a slip' between the curriculum and the pupil. There have been plenty of good approaches to the teaching of literacy – some of these work with some children and some with others. It is always tempting to blame the child for not managing to deal with the curriculum. But the good teacher knows that it is up to the teacher to do what they can to get their class engaged with writing.

Researching children's attitudes

Trying to find out what young children's views are about anything is fraught with difficulty. First of all there is the fact that most children of 5–7 are keen to please adults and to do the right thing. Therefore they may decide to give the answer they think we want rather than any other. As an adult, in school, the researcher is automatically attributed with the label of 'teacher person' which gives rise to a whole set of 'expected' answers. In a previous research project, part of which sought to ascertain the views of children on reading, a considerable amount of time was needed to get the 8-year-old boys beyond talking about school books. After a little while they began to talk about comics and books from home and, only after some while, did a wealth of information come out about reading teletext, classified ads from the local paper, and so on. The interviewers not only needed to give children the time to reach this point but in their responses needed not to sound enthusiastic about the expected school-based reading diet as though that is all there is.

As a research team we needed to think about what children would understand by our use of the term writing. This is an interesting aspect of the research design. We wanted to find out their views about writing but first we needed to think about what their ideas might be and what misconceptions they might bring to their under-standing of our question. The word 'writing' might be interpreted just to mean handwriting; it might mean the particular type of lesson that starts with the teacher saying, 'Today we are going to do some writing'. It is probably unlikely that many children would think of any activity outside of school such as writing a list or texting a friend.

In the Talk to Text project, we interviewed pairs of children both before and after the project. Each pair included a boy and a girl nominated by their teacher as doing well in learning to write, of average ability, or having difficulty. So, six children from each class were interviewed twice over the year of the project. We chose to interview children in pairs as this can be less intimidating for them. There is the disadvantage that if one comes up with an idea the pair can latch onto this idea rather than think-ing for themselves. So much of data collection in research is compromise – tell them too much and they follow your lead; tell them too little and they miss the point. Nevertheless we felt that two children would be more comfortable talking to a stranger than one on their own. The mixed gender pairing ensured that, if we did find a differ-ence in attitude between the genders it would be all the more interesting as it would not have had anything to do with one boy or girl using the opinion that their partner had raised.

In order to get children into thinking about writing, as an introductory activity, we showed them a picture of a group of children sitting around a table, holding pencils and either holding up their hand or actually writing. Also in the picture was an adult, most likely a teacher, who was standing behind the group looking at what they were doing. Two of the children each had a thought bubble coming out of their head. There were no words in the bubbles. After explaining to the pair about what the researchers were doing and why, children were asked to write in a thought bubble what the child in the picture could be thinking.

The interview then followed, asking children about their views on what good writing should be like, what they liked and found easy about writing and what strategies they used when they were writing.[1]

Overall attitudes to writing

Overall the attitudes of these 36 children were more positive than negative. Of all the different things they said about writing both at the beginning and the end of the year of the project there were more positive things than negative (56% positive to 44% negative). Interestingly, the percentages were exactly the same at the end of the year as at the beginning, although there were some differences in what they said.

The sort of things that they said they liked could be split into two types: comments that were focused on the actual piece of writing itself; and those that were focused on the feeling of the writer him or herself. The ones focusing on the

Table 7.1   What children liked about writing

What they liked about writing	I like writing stories because you can put your own words in and make it as long as you like.
	I like it when I write a lot.
	Because … you can write loads of fun things and you can write jokes and stuff.
	Because you can do all sorts of things, weird shapes and do colour writing.
What they liked about being a writer	Well, I kind of like the action of my hand and well I think it's kind of … and I like the way that my hand and I like the feel of the pencil and I like it because it's kind of warm.
	I like writing when I have got it all in my head.
	It's just fun to sit down and do a little bit of writing and you can relax and things and it's nice.

---

[1] Further details of the interview schedules used in the project can be found in Appendix 2.

writer were weighted towards liking writing stories, writing about themselves and holidays, writing poems and being able to choose what they write (see Table 7.1).

There were fewer comments about what they did not like. These comments tended to focus on writing long words, making mistakes and having to do it every day. Although there was the same percentage of negative comments at the end of the year, there were fewer about just not liking writing at all. They were more

Table 7.2   What children did not like about writing

What they didn't like about writing	I enjoy writing numbers more than writing letters.
	I don't really like writing short stories, 'cos as soon as you start you just have to stop again.
	We have to write things that are tricky and long words.
	If I make mistakes sometimes I have to go over it and it makes it all scribbly.
What they didn't like about being a writer	It gets boring. I wish we didn't do writing every day.
	It can make your hand ache.
	I don't like it when I make mistakes.
	I sometimes don't enjoy it because it's hard.

specific about the amount of writing they had to do and how difficult they found it (see Table 7.2).

Clearly these children had things that they liked about writing and things that they did not. It is interesting that many of the comments related to being able to do fun things with writing. Looking at their comments about what they liked, they seem to like having freedom to write about things that interest them and that they see as being fun. The negative comments are more about what makes writing hard work and the constraints of having to do it every day and having to do difficult things.

What is hard about writing

The mechanical aspects of writing are hard for young children. If you have ever tried to copy a script that is unfamiliar to you, you will sympathise. For people brought up with English as their first language, learning a new form of writing such as Russian or Urdu requires you to concentrate very carefully on getting the tiny differences in each letter right. Although the experienced reader and writer of languages that use the same letters as English can differentiate very easily between a b and a d, or between an i and a j, differences between unfamiliar letters are much harder to distinguish. Try to copy some of the following letters using the hand that you do not regularly use (left or right):

پس   ق   گ   Ф   Ψ   Љ   Њ   Ж

This should help you understand why children find that writing makes their hands ache. Several children, when asked about what makes writing hard, mentioned the difficulty of long words, long sentences and long stories. Someone said that they found getting bs and ds the wrong way round made writing hard. Someone else just described it as 'shapes and stuff'. At the end of the year of the project one of the main areas of difficulty was doing joined up writing. Although in the long run joining up writing will make writing quicker to do, in the short term it gave these children something else to struggle with when doing writing.

Spelling was also a huge area of anxiety. One of the main things that these children mentioned as being easy in writing was 'short words'. Unsurprisingly, 'long words' were cited as adding to the difficulty of writing. The sort of things that were mentioned as making writing hard were:

- Words that are hard to spell
- Writing long words
- Writing that you can't sound out
- Sounds like 'ch'
- Writing is hard work
- It's hard to do something you can't really do
- I sometimes don't enjoy writing because it is hard
- Writing it is harder than reading it
- Writing is harder than making things
- It's not always easy for me to remember what to do
- Writing is hard so you have to think for a long time.

But it wasn't just the mechanical aspects of writing that caused the problems. It was also the content of writing. Getting ideas came up again and again when talking about what makes writing hard. Children's comments help us begin to realise that getting ideas for the content of the writing is difficult for some. Many children mentioned that they found 'knowing what to write next' or just 'knowing what to write' was hard. One child said that it was hard 'when you don't know how to write the bits in the middle and you get stuck' and someone else just summed the difficulty up as 'remembering everything'.

What are we learning to do?

Think back to something that you are learning to do or have learned in recent years – drive a car, swim, become a teacher, play squash – in each of these you had a picture in your mind about what you were trying to achieve. You had (have) some idea of the kind of teacher that you wanted (want) to be. You may see yourself beating your partner at squash. There may even have been two elements to your motivation. Learning to drive is not just about sitting behind the wheel, it is also about the potential of being able to get to different places easily and quickly.

It is the same with learning to write. As a teacher it is quite easy to forget the child's motivation as one is so involved with one's own concerns about meeting targets, satisfying parents, covering the curriculum. Listening to what children say about their understanding of what good writing involves can give clues as to how to build on or alter this understanding. What would you expect your class to say about the quality of writing? What would you want them to say? In the same way as teachers, young writers have to balance the needs of the assessment system with the longer-term goals of adult functional, not to mention pleasurable, literacy. Children also have to balance the need to do well in school assessment with any other interest they may have in writing – writing texts like their mum; writing a story like Michael Morpurgo; writing at secondary school like their big brother; writing emails on the computer like their dad; writing letters like their granddad. Do they even think about learning to write in such a holistic way or are they too preoccupied with the minutiae of single letters and words?

Another important outcome of talking to children about their learning is the feedback it gives you about your teaching. Several years ago, early years teachers on the English National Writing Project asked their class what made good writers. Those young children's responses were very revealing. There were very many answers such as, 'having a sharp pencil', 'leaving finger spaces', 'not rubbing out' and 'sitting quietly'. The teachers involved in the National Writing Project were quite shocked at these answers and it made them look very carefully at what they said about children's writing.

What would children in your class say makes a good writer?
Have their answers come from what you say to them?
How could you change what you say to help them have a better idea of what makes a good writer?

The children in the Talk to Text project also focused a lot on the secretarial aspects of writing. Finger spaces were mentioned here too. However, the range of things mentioned was wider than those of the young writers in the 1980s. In the Talk to Text project, good writing was seen as neat, small, with finger spaces, having capital letters and full stops. They also thought it was good if you could read it and there was a lot of it.

Their responses, as well as indicating what they thought were the properties of good writing, showed what they thought the good writer in the classroom was like. At the start of the year of the project, children said that good writers think about their work and take time over it, have good ideas and practise a lot. There were also answers that seemed to show that the child did not really understand what a good writer had to do (see Table 7.3), even though they thought that they could identify the good writers in their class.

How can you judge a good writer?

Another way of looking at the answers about good writing and good writers is to sort them according to the evidence that the child seemed to have used to come to their opinion. Therefore the responses were grouped a second time into four types of response: whether the answer referred to evidence from the teacher (e.g. the teacher says); the physical appearance of the writing (e.g. it's neat); the behaviour of the writer (e.g. she reads her writing through); or the behaviour of the child as a pupil (e.g. she puts her hand up a lot) (see Tables 7.3–7.6).

Table 7.3   What is a good writer?

Good writers think and concentrate	I look at my words and see if they are right.
	Because she is concentrating on her work.
	Because she looks like she is looking down at her piece of paper and she knows what she is doing.
Good writers have lots of ideas	Sometimes I get loads of ideas in my head.
	Good writers have good ideas.
Good writers practise	Good writers write often.
	Good writers practise.
Other people are good writers	Morgan is a good writer because he is good at Maths he must be good at writing.
	She's a good writer 'cos she puts her hand up to answer the teacher.

By referring to the appearance of the writing these children were clearly looking at what is produced and showing concern about the physical activity involved in producing writing. Many children referred to good writing as small or straight or neat. Although these are all useful in terms of presentation and legibility, they do not give any evidence that the child understands writing as a means of communicating ideas.

Those who referred to the behaviour of the writer do at least seem to realise that good writing is produced by the writer. This may seem self evident but it is only a few years since that young child may have brought a piece of what looked like scribble to an adult and asked, 'What does this say?' Understanding that the person who does the writing has some control over its quality is important if the young writer is to make useful progress. Many children referred to things that the writer does such as using wow words, having lots of good ideas or thinking before he or she writes.

Other responses referred to behaviour that was more about how pupils behave in class than about the activity of writing itself. Several children made comments similar to that of the girl who said that she could tell who was a good writer because, 'she is still writing when the others have finished'. One girl commented, 'The good writer is yawning because she is tired from doing a lot of writing'. When asked who the good writers in the class were, many children referred to those who put their hand up. Others commented that the good writers looked like they were working hard.

Overall there were 122 different responses given. Of these, 19% referred to the teacher's judgement, 18% to the behaviour of the child as a pupil, 25% to the appearance of the writing and 38% to the behaviour of the writer. This was the only topic which showed any noticeable difference between views before and after the project. After the year of the Talk to Text project where a focus had been on the process of writing, not only were there twice as many responses but these had shifted considerably towards the writing itself, perhaps indicating an increased understanding of what could and could not be achieved. Surprisingly, there was very little difference between the gender or achievement groups in the answers given. The way these are distributed can be seen in Tables 7.4–7.6. It is, however, interesting to note how little the low achievers called on the teachers' opinions in their judgement of who is a good writer.

Table 7.4   How do you know who is a good writer? Beginning and End of the Project

	Teacher's judgement	Pupil behaviour	Appearance of writing	Writer's behaviour
Beginning	24%	31%	12%	33%
End	16%	11%	31%	42%

Table 7.5   How do you know who is a good writer? Gender

	Teacher's judgement	Pupil behaviour	Appearance of writing	Writer's behaviour
Boys	21%	12%	28%	39%
Girls	18%	23%	21%	38%

Table 7.6   How do you know who is a good writer? Achievement

	Teacher's judgement	Pupil behaviour	Appearance of writing	Writer's behaviour
High achievers	29%	22%	18%	31%
Average achievers	20%	12.5%	27.5%	40%
Low achievers	5%	19%	30%	45%

Some of the responses showed a developing sense of good writing behaviour, 'I check that I have got the right letters' and 'I think before I write'. On the other hand, other children showed less awareness, 'The good writer is yawning because she is tired from doing a lot of writing'. The same girl said she knew she was a good writer 'because the teacher says'.

Learning to write

As well as having an idea of what it is that they are trying to achieve, it is to be hoped that young learners have an idea of how they are going to achieve it. Again, thinking back to things that you have learned, you had strategies for getting better at what you were learning. In fact, it is very likely that when things got too difficult, if you could not see any way of making progress, you would give up on the project. In the same way it is helpful if young writers can see what they need to do in order to get better and understand how to do it.

The young writers in the Talk to Text project were asked how they had learned to write and whether they thought that they could have learned to write without going to school. It is interesting to see how much these children thought that learning to write was something that they had a hand in and could do something about and how much they understood it as something that just happened.

Some children did have a sense of development: that as you got older you were able to do things better. They said things such as:

- Babies just scribble; we can write words
- [You get better by] starting with easy words and then getting harder
- You learn how to do it gradually, a bit at a time
- Learning letters and learning words
- Learning to read helps you to write.

Others, although referring to the idea of development, showed less of a sense of how ability developed. They said things such as:

- As you get bigger you can write better
- [You get better by] getting bigger so you can hold a pencil
- Our brains got bigger
- By becoming intelligent. Like Spiderman – he is intelligent and good at writing.

Literacy is seen as a central part of the school curriculum. The three Rs of reading, writing and 'rithmetic have always been understood as the key things that are learned in school. A surprising element of these children's responses was that teachers did not figure as large in their responses about how they had learned to write as we would have expected. Those children who referred to people as having helped them learn to write mentioned family members as often as they referred to their teachers. They said things like:

- Your parents teach you when you are a baby
- You need a bit of help from teachers when you start off
- You could learn without school when you are five it is easy
- Teachers tell you how to do it and then you do it
- Your mum could teach you.

There were children who did seem to understand that learning and making progress did also come from their own efforts as well as being helped by others and just growing up. Many of these referred to practising as a way of getting better at writing. These children said things such as:

- The more they do the better they get
- I kept learning new words and I found new words
- Looking at the word and writing it
- By doing harder work
- You try your best.

Overall 39% of children's views attributed their development as writers to their own efforts, 45% to someone else and 16% purely to getting older or bigger. How these were distributed among the children can be seen in Tables 7.7 and 7.8. Here the boys were more likely to attribute their learning to their own efforts than to someone else and girls to attribute it to another person. There appeared to be very little difference according to achievement group with the low achievers attributing their learning slightly less to themselves than had children in other groups.

Table 7.7   How do you learn to write? Gender

	Self	Another person	Growing up
Boys	43%	40%	17%
Girls	35%	50%	15%

Table 7.8   How do you learn to write? Achievement

	Self	Another person	Growing up
High achievers	41%	44%	15%
Average achievers	41%	44%	15%
Low achievers	35%	48%	17%

Doing writing

The aim of school must be to help children develop independence. Clearly there would be no future in teaching children to just get better at copying the teacher's writing. They need to be developing ways of solving the problems faced by a writer ultimately without the help of a teacher. Several years ago, young writers in what was then called the infant school, were given word books. Far too much learning and teaching time was spent waiting for the teacher to write the spelling of a particular word in this book. Although not often seen in class-rooms today, it provides a good example of how teaching strategies can support the development of independence or foster dependence.

Compare the difference between the following two scenarios. In the first the child goes to the adult, whether teacher, Teaching Assistant or parent, with a closed book or piece of paper. The adult takes the paper or opens the book at the correct place and writes the word. The child returns to their writing and copies the word. In the second, the child finds the appropriate letter card or page in their personal dictionary, has a go at writing the word as best they can, takes it to the adult who comments on their attempt and then writes the correct version.

The child then returns to their writing, looks at the correct spelling, covers the word and then tries to write it from memory. In the first version, the correct word has found its way onto the child's page but very little learning has taken place. In the second illustration, he or she has begun to learn the rudiments of using a dictionary, has had a go and received feedback on his or her attempt and then made some progress in remembering the word by having to remember the spelling, if only for a very short while. The second version has taken very slightly longer but is supporting the child in moving some way towards independence.

In the Talk to Text project children were asked what helped them when they wrote. Children were asked questions such as 'What do you do when you are stuck?' and 'What helps you when you are writing?'. In order to explore how these children were developing a sense of independence in their approach to writing, the responses were sorted according to the source of the strategies they chose: whether the response referred to themselves (e.g. 'I think'), whether it referred to another person (e.g. the teacher) or whether it referred to a strategy provided within the classroom (e.g. a word card) (see Tables 7.9 and 7.10).

Many children referred to the resources provided in the classroom to help them. These were almost exclusively resources that would help them with spellings. Each classroom had a resource such as a word wall, word wheel, alphabet line, have-a-go cards and so on. Children were familiar with the use of these for help with spelling and, if they referred to a classroom resource, this is what they would refer to. Only two children mentioned getting help with ideas and they both suggested either copying from a book or getting ideas from a book.

Some children referred to their own efforts as helping them with their writing and made statements such as, 'Try and figure it out' and 'Think. Say it over and over in my head'. These children often mentioned that they sounded out the word or, as one said, 'saying words out and guess'. It was also apparent that some self-help strategies were more helpful than others. Those children who only said that they guessed when they did not know how to spell a word seemed to have less idea about what to do when you do not know how to spell a word. Of course, it must be remembered that these children are very young and may not know how to put what they do into words. The child who says they 'just guess' may actually be a child who is already a good speller and their 'guess' actually provides the correct spelling.

On the other hand the low achieving girl who said that when she is stuck she 'can draw a picture' has made a decision that allows her to continue to be involved in some sort of classroom activity but it will not necessarily help her in her development as a writer. Whereas the girl who said, 'Think of other stories that you know' has developed a strategy that may well help her make progress.

It was mostly the teacher who was referred to as the person who helps them with their writing. As a high achieving girl explained, 'Put your hand up and the teacher comes along'. Or, another girl said 'Put your hand up and she comes and fixes it'. Interestingly, in the interviews at the end of the project, which had made extensive use of writing partners, there was no noticeable increase in the number of those who referred to peers as helping them. Only five children mentioned asking a friend, and then it was likely to be, 'Ask everyone on the table and then the teacher'.

More importantly, it would seem that they were aware of the different possibilities and able to exercise preferences. Overall 33% of responses referred to self, 42% to someone else and 25% to a strategy (number of separate responses = 161).

Table 7.9   What helps me write? Gender

	Self	Another person	Strategy
Boys	41%	36%	23%
Girls	26%	49%	25%

Table 7.10   What helps me write? Achievement

	Self	Another person	Strategy
High achievers	25%	48%	27%
Average achievers	37%	37%	26%
Low achievers	38%	42%	20%

It can be seen that boys were more likely to say that they relied on themselves as opposed to girls who referred to someone else, usually the teacher. One high achieving girl, when asked what she did when she was stuck, replied, 'I just carry on and the teacher will tell you your mistakes'. Whereas some boys made responses such as, 'I just cross it out' or 'I sound it out and think'.

What do you think?

How independent do you think the children are in your class?
What strategies do your children use to help them be independent when they write?
What do you say to help them develop independence?

Interestingly, the high achieving writers were less likely to rely on themselves than the other groups. The low achievers referred less frequently to classroom strategies such as word banks or alphabet friezes as a way of helping them with their writing. A few children also complained that sometimes the teacher would not help.

Although the extent to which these young writers relied on themselves or others in their writing is of interest, the quality of the strategy is also relevant. Some children gave replies such as, 'Someone telling me what letters to write'. On the other hand, others were developing more focused strategies, for example, 'Well if we are writing an ... information piece of writing we can look in the information books that we've got out on display'.

Passivity

One important finding that came from our analysis of children's responses in the interviews about writing was that there was a real difference between the sort of answers that children gave. There was one set of children who gave what appeared to be largely passive responses. These children said that they thought that you got better at writing just by getting older or bigger. When talking about what helps them write, the sort of comments they made were ones that relied on the chance of a teacher coming along or them finding something that they weren't meant to see that would tell them what to write. When asked what they did when they were stuck, they were most likely to say that they waited until someone came and told them what to do. One even said that they waited until they got home and asked their mum.

To illustrate this, we can take two children. One is Tom who provided the picture of an unengaged writer at the start of this chapter. His responses in interview exemplify the type of unhelpful responses where a passive reliance on himself seems unlikely to support him in his development as a writer. Despite being identified by the teacher as one of the low achievers in writing, he said that he considers himself a good writer because he writes fast and very small. (Video evidence of Tom writing confirms the size of his writing but not the speed.) The importance of very small writing was a theme through both his interview sessions. He identified a child in the pictures of children writing used at the start of the interview as being good at writing because he, 'listens to the teacher and never talks'. When asked how he learned to write, he responded, 'As you get bigger you can write better' and 'when you are so young you just do scribbles and as you get bigger you can write better'. In response to the query about what he found helpful he replied, 'What helps me is if someone's telling me what letters I have to do and then I can just write it'. In the second set of interviews he said, 'I quite like it when people [teachers] say that they are not going to leave anything up [on the whiteboard] but they just forget it so that I can copy it'. When stuck he said, 'I basically just try and read it' and even when given other suggestions as to what he might do he replied, 'not really'.

Megan seemed a confident writer who said she knew that she wrote well because, 'I wrote a story and the teacher said it was excellent and she give me a sticker'. However she also said that she thought she was better at Maths. She showed an interesting insight into her attitude to school when she was asked what the children writing in the picture were thinking and she said that the girl in the picture was thinking about, 'what she's going to do after school and who is she going to play with in the playground'. Megan chose the child in the picture as being a good writer 'because she looks like she is looking down at her piece of paper and she knows what she is doing'. When asked how she learned to write, she responded, 'by going to school' and, 'think about it really hard and before you write it in neat write it with your finger'. (The magic finger is a strategy developed as part of the project in which children 'shadow write' a sentence first with their finger as a form of oral rehearsal) In response to the query about what she finds helpful in writing she said, 'we've got these little 'have-a-go' cards, you have a go and see if it looks like the proper word … and [they have] capitals and short words that you use quite often'. And when stuck she told the researcher 'before we ask the teacher we ask everybody on our table … but if they don't know then we ask the teacher'.

Listening to what children can tell us about what they understand about classroom life is often very revealing. It tells us something about how they are interpreting what they see and hear happening around them. It can also help their teachers think about how what teachers say to children and what they provide for children can influence what those children do and think.

Summary of points for the class teacher

> For beginning writers, the secretarial aspects of writing are most important. Teachers can help children understand that there is more to writing than just getting the words and full stops right.
> The things that children understand about writing often come directly from the sort of feedback that their teachers give them.
> Not all children are sure of what they need to do to get better at writing. Teachers can help them understand what they can do.
> Some children adopt a very passive attitude to writing and seem to just wait for someone to help them. Teachers can make sure there are resources in the classroom that support children as they write – and that children know when and how to use them.

Suggested further reading 📖

Bourne, J. (2002) '"Oh, What will Miss Say!" Constructing Texts and Identities in the Discursive Processes of Classroom Writing', *Language and Education*, 16(4): 241–59.

Fisher, R. (2010) 'Young Writers' Construction of Agency', *Journal of Early Childhood Literacy*, 10: 4.

Grainger, T., Goouch, K. and Lambirth, A. (2002) 'The Voice of the Child: "We're Writers" Project', *Reading: Literacy and Language*, 36(3): 135–9.

Merisuo-Storm, T. (2006) 'Girls and Boys Like to Read and Write Different Texts', *Scandinavian Journal of Educational Research*, 50(2): 111–25.

Pajares. F. and Valiante, G. (1999) 'Influence of Writing Self-efficacy Beliefs on the Writing Performance of Upper Elementary Students', *Journal of Educational Research*, 90: 353–60.

Turner, J. and Scott, G. (1995) 'How Literacy Tasks Influence Children's Motivation for Literacy', *The Reading Teacher*, 48(8): 662.

Lesson plans for reflection

Reflection Activity – Evaluating Writing

Purpose: To encourage reflection about the process of writing.

Summary: Children use a checklist to help them evaluate their writing.

Resources/preparation: A recent piece of individual writing.

Activity

- During shared writing the teacher and children draw up a list of the questions to ask about their writing, and how they write.

Ideas for focus questions

What kind of writing is this? How do we know?
Where did you get your ideas from?
What were you trying to write about?
How well did you write about this?
What did you do when you got stuck?
What were you thinking about when you were writing this?
What were you feeling when you wrote this?
Could you have done it differently?

- The teacher shares a piece of work they have written and models talking about the process of writing using the focus questions.
- The children work in pairs and talk about a piece of their own writing using the focus questions.

Class-based example

A Year 3 class have been working with their teacher Jan on a Design and Technology project to make healthy sandwiches. During the week they have designed, made and tested their sandwiches and written instructions for making their sandwich. Jan gathers the class on the carpet and explains that they are going to be thinking about the writing they have done. She has a list of focus questions that the children generated during a previous session. Together they choose three questions that are appropriate to the instruction writing. 'Where did you get your ideas from?', 'What did you do when you got stuck?' and 'Could you have done it differently?'

Jan shows the children a set of instructions she has written and models reflecting on the first two questions. The children then have time to share their piece of writing with a partner and reflect on the questions. The children gather for a plenary to talk about their ideas.

If this is the first time you have tried this activity …

- Remember that children are often unfamiliar with this level of reflection.
- They may need plenty of modelling before they are ready to engage in this kind of activity in pairs.

Encouraging reflection

Try saying 'Tell me about …' rather than 'Why?'
'How was that the same as …?'
'When you said … it really helped me understand your thinking.'

Reflection Activity – A Step-by-Step Writing Guide

Purpose: To encourage reflection about the process of writing in a particular genre. A greater awareness of the writing process may help children to become more critical of their writing and more self reliant in terms of producing written work.

Summary: Children reflect on the skills they use to write in a particular genre and create a step-by-step writing guide for other children to use.

Resources/preparation:

- Sugar paper, scissors, glue.
- A genre with which the children are very familiar.

Activity

- Chose a genre with which the children are very familiar, e.g. story.
- Tell the children they are going to produce a writing guide for other children to use.
- In pairs children discuss how they go about writing a story and note their ideas on sugar paper.
- When they have enough ideas the children cut out each idea and order their thoughts, putting the most important first, creating a poster as they go.
- Writing guides are shared at the plenary with plenty of time built in for differing ideas.
- Posters are delivered to their target audience so the children see that their writing had a real audience and purpose.

Class-based example

Leah works with a class of 30 Year 2 children. They have been working on stories with familiar settings and have engaged in lots of shared and individual story writing. Leah now wants to encourage the children to reflect on their work and to see what they have learned about story writing during their unit of work. She explains that the children in Year 1 are going to be writing some stories, but they are not as experienced story writers as the children in Year 2 so they need some help. Leah's class will be writing a step-by-step story writing guide. In pairs, the children talk about what they do when they write a story. They share these ideas and then move to their tables in pairs to note down their ideas. As the activity is underway Leah monitors progress. She finds that some of the children are struggling with this activity. Many are sidetracked into describing stories they have written rather than focusing on how to write a story. Leah encourages them to think about the purpose and audience of their writing. **What** are we writing? **Who** are we writing it for? **Why** are we writing it? She uses careful questioning to draw out their ideas about the process of writing.

During the plenary Leah shares the guides that children have written. Together they think about:

- What helped you to do this?
- What made it difficult?
- How did you work together?

If this is the first time you have tried this activity …

- Remember that reflection is a skill that children can sometimes find challenging. When you begin this kind of reflection include plenty of teacher modelling so children learn how to reflect on **process** as well as product.

Teachers who use this activity successfully might say:

'Tell me the first thing you think about when you begin to write a story'
'Tell me how you make sure people understand your story'
'What is tricky about writing stories?'
'When you are writing a story, what do you do now that you couldn't do in Year 1?'
'Are you finding it easy or difficult to think about how you write stories? Tell me more …'

Reflection Activity – Thinking Cap

Purpose: To encourage reflection about the process of writing.

Summary: Children wear a 'thinking cap' to help them focus on reflective questions about their writing.

Resources/preparation:

- A class set of 'thinking caps' or hats.
- A recent piece of individual writing.

Activity

- The thinking cap is an actual cap that the teacher or a pupil can wear. The teacher explains to the children that wearing the cap can help you to think about your writing.
- Each child has a recent piece of writing.
- In pairs they take turns to wear the 'thinking cap' and talk to their partner about their writing. The aim is to focus on process rather than product.

Ideas for focus questions

What kind of writing is this?
Where did you get your ideas from?
What were you trying to write about?
How well did you write about this?
What did you do when you got stuck?
What were you thinking about when you were writing this?
What were you feeling when you wrote this?
Could you have done it differently?

Class-based example

Graham has been working with his class of 25 Year 2 children. They have been writing kennings about jungle animals. Graham returns to the shared writing they completed in the last session – a kenning about a monkey. He shows the children the thinking cap and explains that while he is wearing it, he is able to think really carefully about his writing. He has three prompt questions on cards: 'What kind of writing is this?', 'What did you do when you got stuck?' and 'What were you feeling when you wrote this?'. Graham models wearing the thinking cap and explaining his ideas carefully. He then asks children to return to their desks. They will be working in pairs talking about their own kennings. Each pair has a 'thinking cap' and they take it in turns to talk about their writing whilst wearing the cap. At the end of the shared talk activity each child writes down one thing that the 'thinking cap' helped them reflect upon. In the plenary Graham looks at the children's written reflections and reinforces the importance of reflection.

If this is the first time you have tried this activity …

- Remember that children are often unfamiliar with this level of reflection.
- Begin by using the 'thinking cap' as part of shared writing sessions. Model the things **you** might say while **you** are wearing the 'thinking cap'. Next ask children to wear the 'thinking cap' and help them to reflect on their writing. When you are happy that they are gaining confidence with this activity then move on to using the 'thinking cap' in pairs.

Teachers who use this activity successfully might say:

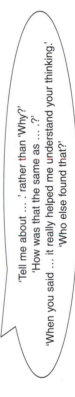

'Tell me about … ' rather than 'Why?'
'How was that the same as … ?'
'When you said … it really helped me understand your thinking.'
'Who else found that?'

Reflection Activity – Two Ticks and a Wish

Purpose: To encourage reflection about the content of a piece of writing.

Summary: Children reflect on a piece of writing and find two things that are positive and one thing that could be improved.

Resources/preparation: A recent piece of individual writing.

Activity

- During shared work, look at a recent piece of writing.
- Explain that you are going to be thinking about 'two ticks and a wish'. This means that you will be looking for two parts of the writing that are really good, and one thing that could be improved.
- Put two ticks next to the parts of the writing that are really good (perhaps linked to the learning objective).
- In a cloud shape at the bottom of the writing write down a wish, or one thing that could be improved.

Class-based example

Lucy found that when she asked her Year 1 class to talk about the content of their written work, their comments were very general. They said things like, 'It's nice', 'I like it', 'It's neat', 'It's too hard', 'It's untidy'. Lucy wanted to improve the writing of the children in her class. She decided to encourage her pupils to evaluate their work in a more specific way.

The class were writing a recount of a class visit. Lucy decided to introduce the idea of 'two ticks and a wish'. On Monday and Tuesday during shared writing, Lucy's class began to write a recount of a farm visit. At the end of each shared writing session Lucy modelled 'two ticks and a wish'. At this point she merely demonstrated with a focus on important language.

On Wednesday, the children were writing independently about the farm machinery they saw during their visit. At the end of their writing, Lucy asked the children to re-read what they had written and talk about 'two ticks and a wish' with a partner. She repeated this on Thursday and Friday. By the end of the week many children were being more specific in their oral evaluations. In the following weeks Lucy helped the children to develop their oral evaluations. By the end of the half term most of the children were able to use 'two ticks and a wish' as an independent self-evaluation strategy.

Extension activity

If you are working with older or more able children who are confident at using 'two ticks and a wish', encourage them to mark each other's work on Post-it notes. Continue to emphasise the need for **specific** feedback.

Teachers who use this activity successfully say things like:

'This word is really good because …'
'This sentence starts with a really good connective …'
'The punctuation in this bit helps me to understand the writing.'
'This phrase is excellent because …'
'The part I think I would like to change is … because …'
'To make it even better I think I will …'

8 Managing Talk for Writing in the Classroom

Ros Fisher

Introduction

So far in this book we have considered what previous research has shown us about the relationship between talk and writing. We have looked at how undertaking research can help you in your role, whether as a class teacher or otherwise involved in working in schools. We have also looked very carefully at how the three different strategic elements of talk worked with children in the classroom. We have examined how this talk can come through in their writing and we have also reported what children told us about what they think about writing. For the final chapter, the focus turns to the teacher.

We worked with six excellent teachers on the project. They came with varying degrees of experience – from one in her first year of teaching to others with more than 20 years' experience. Each one brought superb ideas for engaging children in writing and first-class skills in managing children in the classroom. Each of the six classrooms were happy, lively places with children eager to learn. Nevertheless, they were real teachers in real classrooms with real children.

Anyone who has spent time as a teacher and as an observer in a classroom will know that it is the easiest thing to be critical of the teacher when you are sitting at the back watching. Most of the examples given in this chapter are illustrations of teacher practice that worked well to give you the opportunity to reflect on how such practice might be useful to you. Where there is implied criticism, it is not intended to be criticism of the teacher herself but of a particular incidence of practice that could have been different.

Managing talk

Clarifying the purpose of the talk

In the Talk to Text project we identified three purposes for the talk: to generate ideas; to rehearse the form of the text; and to reflect. This definition of three separate purposes is new. Most texts that emphasise the importance of talk for writing do not separate the different purposes. Our research showed us that this clarity of purpose is important. Talk to generate ideas aims to provide a range of ideas for the content of writing. It is likely to cover a large part or the whole of the composition. This use of talk allows children to choose from a range of ideas that they or their peers have suggested. On the other hand talk for oral rehearsal is more limiting. It operates mainly at sentence level and is about the best way to express one of the ideas for content. The teachers coined the phrase 'short burst writing' for the sort of writing that was most suitable for oral rehearsal. Talk for reflection can take place at any time but its purpose is to help young writers become aware of how writers think and act.

These three separate strategic elements have different purposes. If these purposes are to be well served, how they are managed is important.

Starting to write

The teacher's quote used in Chapter 3 (p. 48) bemoaned the fact that although the talk children undertook before writing was good, so often it did not come through into their writing. Teachers in the Talk to Text project emphasised the importance of planning for the change from a talk context to a writing context. So often it can happen that the movement from carpet to table, collecting paper and pencils, arguing over seating and so on results in all the ideas being forgotten. Some useful things to think about in your planning might be:

- Plan for where the children will be sitting for the talk. If they are on the carpet, how will you finish the talk to make sure they do not lose their ideas between carpet and desk? If they are at their tables, how will you ensure that they don't fiddle with any resources already on the tables?

- Are all the resources needed for the writing available to be given to children quickly? Make sure that you don't allocate this task to children. They may then lose the benefit of the talk activities while giving out the resources.

- Make sure that the last thing you say to the class is about what you want them to do. Reminding them that they need to work hard as there is PE next, may not help retain the ideas from the talk. How you explain the task to children, in particular the last point that you make, can be very influential in what they take as being your real purpose. All the wonderful talk about interesting ideas or exciting words can be lost if the last thing that they hear is about full stops or finger spaces.

Easy tasks: difficult tasks

A fascinating insight into classroom practice from the Talk to Text videos was about the nature of the tasks set by teachers. The teachers worked hard to motivate these young writers and to set tasks that were manageable and meaningful.

It was interesting to reflect on why these sometimes went wrong. A good example here is a lesson about healthy eating with a group of 5–6-year-olds. Children were asked to make a list of things that made them healthy. The talk centred around healthy foods such as carrots and fruit and around healthy activities such as exercise and fresh air. They had obviously discussed this before and children came up with plenty of ideas. The trouble started with the writing task. The teacher tried to make the task more simple by saying that they just needed to write a list. They didn't need to write a sentence but a simple statement like 'eating carrots' would be fine. Unfortunately these children were far too well versed in the importance of sentences with full stops and capital letters. The more the teacher tried to reassure them that just a couple of words would be fine, the more confused they became. Here the simplification of the task had moved so far from children's expectation of a writing task that it was actually more demanding of them! In another lesson children were talking about farming and they were asked to label a picture of a tractor. Here the task was more straightforward for them as they had looked at other labelled diagrams in preparation and were happy to write single words as labels.

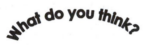

Do you need to reconsider how you set tasks?
What are the best ways that you have found to arrange groups for talk?
Could you try taping your introduction to writing and see whether you emphasise what you think you do?

Prompts to support talk for writing

Talking is easy. Much time is spent in classrooms trying to stop children talking instead of working. In these classrooms, talk was important. It was used to support children's efforts at writing. However, it is not always easy to get children to talk about *what* we want them to and *in the way* that we want them to. In the Talk to Text project various different kinds of prompts were tried to help focus children on the talk task.

Puppets

Several of the talk activities involved the pairs of children being involved in role play. Provided enough had been done to set the scene and the roles were well understood, this worked well. In some activities, teachers also provided very basic puppets to support the role play. These can be made very easily as cut outs from children's drawings or paper rings to use as finger puppets with a simple face drawn on. These very straightforward props seemed to be just enough to keep the focus on the character whose talk will become the writing.

Prompt sheets

Cards or photocopied sheets made specifically for a particular task can also be helpful. Often no more than three simple questions introduced at the start of the lesson and put on each table were enough to support children as they talked or wrote. In one role play before writing about animals under threat of extinction the paper held the following three questions. These questions acted as a prompt for the role play and a scaffold for the writing. Less experienced writers used some of the boxes to draw in instead of writing.

Who are you?	Where do you live?	Why are you becoming extinct?
A seal	The sea	The fisherman are killing me.
An elephant	Africa	They hunt me for my tusks.

Another teacher used the questions:

- What do you see?
- What do you hear?
- What do you feel?

These helped children as they wrote about a boy riding his bike really fast for the first time.

Paper shaped like a speech bubble helped some children when they had to write what their character had said during the role play.

Maps

The class that wrote a simple poem about a walk around their neighbourhood, started by producing a simple map of the places they planned to visit. The map was no more than a shape with places marked on it. However, the decision making involved in deciding what to include and in what order served well to focus the talk on the content of the writing that would follow.

Maps can be used in other ways. They do not have to be of places that children know. Story maps can be really useful in helping children to work out what happens in a story. Think about the maps that could be drawn for *Little Red Riding Hood*, *The Three Little Pigs*, and so on. One class had a 3D model of a forest with the characters from *Little Red Riding Hood*. Opportunities for talk during play with this model fed into writing about Little Red Riding Hood and other characters having adventures in a forest.

Planning for talk

Whole-class talk

Holding a discussion with 30 people is not easy. It is made more difficult when 29 of those people are very young. Inevitably there has to be some control of who talks, when, what about and for how long. A great deal has been written about the way in which much of what happens in whole-class discussion tends to lead to a question and answer session with the teacher doing most of the talking and leading the topic and direction of the talk. There are however other ways in which whole-class talk could be planned to avoid the normal pattern of initiation, response, feedback (IRF).

Teacher-in-role
Here, by being in-role as someone other than the teacher, you can overturn the normal pattern. By taking the role of a character in a story, children can be given freedom to pose the teacher questions instead of the other way around which is more normal. Other roles that can work are that of author or expert on a particular topic. See Chapter 3 for more about teacher-in-role.

Pupil-in-role
Provided you have done enough teacher-in-role so that children understand about this kind of role play, there is no reason why a child cannot take the place of the teacher and adopt a role. Here they could be a character from a story with a dilemma and they could ask the rest of the class for advice. As they get more experienced they could take the role of a character in their own story. Responding to questions from peers about their story will help them develop their understanding of the relationship between reader and writer. Clearly this is a more advanced form of role play and children will have had to have some experience before trying this.

Circle time
Sitting children in a circle with a 'magic microphone' or similar device that allows each child to talk in turn is another way of undermining the dominant

role of the teacher in whole-class talk. However, what results is not a discussion. In normal interaction speakers respond to each other and the dialogue builds with responses going back and forth. In a circle, each speaker has their say. It does not necessarily have to follow on from what the previous person has said. This works well for 'short burst' writing. At a very simple level, a circle with each child saying what is their favourite animal and why gives plenty of ideas for the writer and plenty of opportunity to orally rehearse what they are going to write.

In the Talk to Text project, one teacher had the good idea of trying to get her class to compose a story in a circle. She put out two cards: a character card and a setting card. On the character card she put Spenser the Bear and on the setting card she put some sand. The story was about Spenser going to the beach. After the whole-class session the children went off in pairs to write their own paired stories. The paired writing worked well and some good stories were produced. However, the creation of a cumulative story, while quite good fun for all involved, resulted in no more than a series of statements about what Spenser did. These young children were not able to sustain the story line through 28 different turns. However, the often unrelated statements that they did come up with fed into the stories that they went off later to write.

Paired talk

In whole-class sessions
Brief interludes of paired talk within whole-class sessions is now widely used. This has the benefit of breaking up a time when, otherwise, some children may sit for an extended length of time without contributing. Not all children (or even adults) are happy talking in front of a large group. These episodes can be just a couple of minutes long or longer. It is easier to either have children sit ready in pre-determined pairs or to get them to talk with the child nearest them. It is best to avoid lengthy and disruptive moving around during the lesson as it detracts from the focus that you are wanting to achieve. These paired talk sessions can be very open ended with a starter such as 'What do you think will happen next?' Such topics are useful for giving children confidence in their own ideas but can be daunting for those with less to say. Alternatively, topics for talk can be very tightly structured, such as, 'I want you to decide where the train went next'. Paired talk in carpet-based whole-class sessions is likely to be more geared to idea generation or reflection than oral rehearsal.

Just before and during writing
Paired talk just before or during writing is more likely to be for oral rehearsal. Here the talk can help beginning writers craft the words they want to use with help from a friend at the point of writing. Such talk is described in detail in Chapter 4.

The Giant Postman – paired talk in action

In the lesson based on *The Giant Postman* described in Chapter 5, the teacher makes good use of paired talk in the whole-class part of the lesson. The story is used to set up the writing task of completing the story. The giant postman is causing a disturbance in the village when he delivers the letters so Billy decides that he will write to him to ask him to be more careful and he will deliver the letter himself. The teacher began by reading the first part of the story which tells of the disruption caused by the giant postman and sets the context for writing the letter. She opens the first session of paired talk with, 'What do you think?' They found this difficult. It is a good example of where an open ended question does not always give enough guidance for talk. At first there was little talk until the teacher gave help with prompts from the story to encourage them to come up with ideas for what people might be feeling.

In the next part of the lesson, the teacher wonders aloud what Billy might say in his letter. This stimulates more talk. Wondering aloud is a useful strategy for encouraging talk. Children are used to questions from the teacher and these questions often have a right answer; one the teacher knows and the children must find. By wondering aloud you imply that you do not know the answer. This then leaves an opening for the children to put forward their ideas more freely.

Next she explained to the class that she did not know what happened next and asked the children to think what might happen. This episode of paired talk was more structured. The children were given three questions to focus their talk: 'When did Billy go to the giant's house?', 'How was Billy feeling?' and 'What problem did he find when he got there?' She then gave the children one minute to come up with an answer to the first question, another minute for the second question and another for the third. Between talking about each question, children fed back their answers.

In this one lesson three forms of paired talk have been used. One used a very open starting point. One opened with the teacher wondering aloud but on the specific problem of what Billy might write. The third was very focused and structured with specific questions. These three questions then led into the writing task. The writing that two of the children produced from this lesson can be seen on p. 96.

Although the highly structured paired talk episodes produced more talk and more relevant talk, this should not be seen as implying that such talk tasks are better. Children need to experience a variety of opportunities. It is good that there should be some talk tasks that are more open. These allow children to develop their own ideas and to gain a sense of ownership of the writing that follows. The more focused talk tasks before children started to write helped them move from the idea generation stage into what was more like oral rehearsal in preparation for writing.

Who else?

In some of the Talk to Text classes the use of paired talk became so embedded that teachers encouraged the use of toys as partners for talk. For some children the pairing with a toy was immensely helpful. Whether because of the novelty or whether because of the uncritical nature of their partner, for some children and particularly those who were struggling with writing, this was a very supportive resource. In fact, one boy was able to achieve a very unexpected Level 2 in his writing assessment at the end of Year 2 by being allowed to take his toy with him and talk to it while writing. A lesson plan based on 'Talk to a Toy' can be found earlier in the book in the section of lessons for write aloud p. 106.

Group talk

Although most of the talk in the Talk to Text project was either as a whole class or in pairs, there is no reason why other groupings should not also be used. Predominantly, groups of more than two are likely to be for idea generation or reflection. Oral rehearsal, coming as it does just before writing, is better conducted as a pair. Its purpose is to help the young writer craft the sentence just before writing. Too many versions will only be confusing and increase cognitive load rather than reducing it.

Groups of three are very useful in discussion-based talk. The threesome allows one of the group to sit back and think before contributing. It can reduce the likelihood of one child in a pair dominating. The third contributor also provides an extra source of ideas. With groups of three or more it is possible to allocate roles for the talk: notetaker, chair, observer, and so on. All this adds variety to the talk. However, it is important not to lose sight of the purpose of the talk as supporting writing. Too many children, too many ideas, too much talk could result in adding to cognitive load rather than reducing it.

Grouping for talk

One aspect of the practice of encouraging pupil talk that was evident at the beginning of the Talk to Text project was that some children did not like to be allocated a particular child to talk with. For the purposes of the research, we had decided to use boy–girl pairs with children whom their teachers had nominated according to their achievement in writing. Some videos from early in the project show a real reluctance for one child to have to talk to their designated partner rather than their friend. Whether this was from a reluctance to work with someone of the opposite gender or whether it was because they wanted to talk to friends was not clear. Nevertheless, this was only evident early on in the project. After a few weeks they got quite used to working with their 'talk partner' and the pairings worked well.

Again for purposes of the research we opted for pairings of children who were roughly the same in their level of writing achievement. This was helpful for the research as it enabled us to see whether certain types of talk were more likely to occur with high or low achieving writers. However, mixed pairs also have their place. It can be particularly helpful to place a child who lacks ideas with one who has plenty; a child who is brimming with ideas with one who is good at focusing on the task at hand. Having one scribe in a group of two or three can give struggling writers the chance to experience composition in a way that would not be possible if they were doing the writing themselves.

Teacher talk

In the previous chapter we heard what the children told us about writing. One aspect that came through clearly was that spelling, punctuation and handwriting stood out as areas of real importance for these young writers. As has been seen in the discussion at the beginning of this book, there are reasons to do with how the brain works that make this preoccupation inevitable as children cope with the range of demands placed on them by the conventions of reproducing written language. However, as teachers we want children to understand more about writing than just these secretarial aspects – important as they are. In the following section, a lesson introduction is described. Whilst the ideas and topic were promising, certain aspects of the planning and introduction detracted from its success.

This teacher regularly used a large bird puppet called Whistling Winnie. On this morning the children were very excited as Winnie had written a letter to the class during the night. The letter invited them to write to him and tell him all about themselves. He describes how he loves eating insects and slugs which caused great excitement from both teacher and children. In his letter he invites children to write back to him. He writes,

> You could ask a question in your letter. I spoke to your teacher about giving a prize for the neatest letter and the hardest worker. I wanted to give you lovely juicy beetles but your teacher said you may prefer stickers. What do you think? I hope to hear from you soon.
>
> Love from Whistling Winnie

After reading the letter and discussing how exciting it was to get a letter from Winnie, the teacher asked children what they might write in their letters to Winnie. Having established that the letter would start with 'Dear Winnie', the teacher then asked 'What else do you want to put in your letter?' The children's answers were revealing:

- Alliteration
- Neat writing
- Finger spaces

The teacher's response to these suggestions was 'Brilliant!'.

What have the children in this class learned about writing? The teacher had set up the lesson to motivate her class to be interested in the writing task and to give them a 'genuine' audience to write for. She had clearly been successful in getting the class excited. They were all really keen to contribute ideas. They did all seem as though they wanted to write a letter to Winnie. But their answers show what they have learned about what is important in writing: it is not what is interesting but what it looks like and, we suspect, the most recent topic in their lessons: alliteration. Even Winnie's name gives us a clue that this may be a recent topic. Indeed, the letter itself gives a further clue as to what this teacher thinks is important. Winnie's prize will be for 'the neatest letter and the hardest worker'.

Here it seems that the way the lesson has been set up and the feedback given to the children, rather than focusing on the stated intention of encouraging motivation and considering audience, in fact highlighted mainly secretarial aspects of writing. This is made all the more interesting by what this teacher said about the Talk to Text project at the end of the year. She was very enthusiastic and said that she had enjoyed the work immensely, but she had some concerns.

> I think that the project helped them to get the creative ideas and the quantity was definitely there. But I feel I need to do much more work on the sort of structured handwriting and spelling and the things they are getting marks for like that, punctuation and letter formation, things like that, because we were being quite experimental and imaginative, they got that side beautifully …

It is interesting to note that the very things that she seemed to emphasise in her interaction with children were what she most felt that she had neglected.

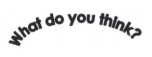

> Do you have something that you worry about neglecting in your teaching?
> How aware are your class of this?
> How would you re-plan this lesson to avoid giving an unintended impression?

Giving instructions

In the example above, despite what the teacher had planned to achieve from the lesson, the way in which she interacted with the children at the start of the lesson and even what the 'bird' had written in the letter, placed the emphasis elsewhere. In other lessons, the impact of a really interesting introductory session with talk that generated lots of ideas for writing was marred by the final remarks being about full stops, capital letters or spelling.

In the Talk to Text project, this problem was mostly avoided by the oral rehearsal phase of the lesson. Children talked in their pairs before writing. Their talk was focused on the words they were going to write immediately before they wrote.

This did not mean that these teachers neglected the secretarial aspects of writing. They had separate handwriting and spelling sessions. Checking for spelling and punctuation was relegated to the end of a writing session when children were encouraged to check what they had written for correct spelling and punctuation.

Scaffolding writing

Once children had started writing the type of interaction between teacher and writer will also impact on what seems to be valued. Several years ago in another research project the researchers described a writing lesson in which children were asked to write an imaginative piece about volcanoes. The introduction focused on the excitement of volcanoes and the potential creativity of the writing. There was even a working model of a volcano. However, all the comments made by the teacher during the lesson concentrated on the neatness and tidiness of the writing. The writing that pupils produced gained praise from the teacher despite being no more than quite predictable short accounts of the demonstration. To the research team this writing did not seem to be what had been asked for. The children in the class knew otherwise (Desforges et al., 1985).

In a Year 1 class, the children were writing in response to the story of *Billywise* by Judith Nicholls. In the story Billywise, a young owl, has to learn to fly. His mother tries to give him the courage to fly but he is scared. The class had used talk activities to think about what Billywise might be thinking and what his mother might say to him to encourage him to dare. As the teacher went around the class and spoke to individual children about their writing, she read out what they had written and then commented. These comments responded to the intended meaning of the writing rather than the appearance of the writing. One child had written for Billywise 'It's too scarey'. The teacher read this out in a quavering, frightened voice then said eagerly, 'Yes that's good'. Another child had put the mother as saying 'Just do it'. This was read aloud with some exasperation and then the teacher said 'I like that'.

In another class the children were writing a story and they had been asked to try to use some interesting words. As the teacher went around seeing what the children had written, she picked out individual words or phrases and commented on the interesting words, saying things like. 'I like your *slippery*' and 'Oh, *tickly* is good'. Here the comments were clearly focused on what the children had been asked to do. However, see the section below for the danger of giving the impression that some words are good in their own right instead of being good in the context of that piece of writing.

Choosing words

The choice of words seems to be a key part of many teachers' work with children prior to writing. Large sections of interaction that we observed on the Talk to Text project involved teachers helping children think of different words to use in their writing. The focus was either on avoiding the most obvious word or on thinking up more intense words – as with the child who suggested 'petrified' in the earlier example. The notion of 'powerful words' was often used in the encouragement to use a wider range of word choice. However, the way in which these ideas were introduced varied in method and in effectiveness.

Words are not powerful in their own right – their power lies in the way they are used. A classic example of this came during a lesson in which children were collaboratively composing a story from a collection of objects. First of all they had sat in a circle on the carpet and taken it in turns to add a sentence to the cumulative story. The result was not a great story but each child had contributed something and everyone had heard a great many ideas that they could take and use for themselves. Children then talked in pairs to make up a story. After a few minutes, the teacher stopped them and asked for some ideas. The dialogue went as follows:

Child 1   I went to the beach and it was sunny.

Child 2   I came back from the beach and I saw a single pebble.

Child 3   I went into my house and found some sandwiches.

Teacher   Has it got an exciting word in it?

Child 3   I went into my extremely hot house and found some yummy sandwiches.

Teacher   Brilliant.

Although 'extremely hot' and 'yummy' have been added, whether they contribute anything to the quality of the writing is questionable.

Children then went to their tables and had a go at writing their own story. One child wrote a very simple story about going to the beach and having some sandwiches. Rather than commenting on the overall impression of the story, the teacher homed in immediately on one sentence:

Teacher   In it you said it was sunny and you had lunch. But when you were doing lunchtime and you were talking about the food I would really like to have known what it tastes like, alright. So instead of just saying I had a sandwich tell me what it tastes like. What does it taste like?

Child   Chicken.

Teacher   Chicken? It tastes like chicken [laughs].

The child here has responded to the teacher's question in a literal way. The question has not sought to improve the sense of the writing and the answer has done no more than provide more information.

Here words seem to be treated as though some are better than others regardless of what they do in the sentence or within the whole text. In a story in which there is a sentence, 'I went into my house and found some sandwiches', the insertion of an adjective is unlikely to make the narrative more compelling. The second excerpt of dialogue illustrates the fact that the children have not really understood what is expected of them. When asked what the sandwich tastes like, a literal answer, 'Chicken' is given. The children are clearly working hard to give the teacher what she is asking for but they do not seem to have any sense of why she wants this extra information.

In contrast, another teacher who was working with children to create a description of what it feels like when riding a bike, went about it in a very different way. This is the second lesson in which the writing has been based on a story about a child learning to ride his bike. The teacher asked the children to close their eyes and imagine they are on the bike and riding fast. She asked them to think about what they could see, what they could hear and what did they feel.

Teacher	When you've thought of some really good words you can sit up. I'll write a few of them up here for ideas and then you can go away and do your own.
Child 1	I can hear the wind whistling.
Teacher	I can hear the wind whistling – good girl. I can hear the wind whistling. Good description. Any other ideas?
Child 2	I can see the blurry trees.
Teacher	Good, excellent. Why are they blurry, who can tell me - it's a really good word but why are they blurry?
Child 3	They are going so fast.
Teacher	They are going so fast. They are rushing past.
Child 4	I can see the bushes go past.
Teacher	I can see the bushes go past – but that's not quite so expressive. We've got a 'hear' and a 'see' has anyone got a 'feel' they can give me?
Child 5	I can feel the air brushing against my face.
Teacher	Ooh lovely I can feel the air brushing, good word, against my face. Super ideas.

At the end of the lesson, when children have written their own descriptive sentences about riding the bike, they are asked to pick out their best sentence. As children read out their best sentence, they are also asked to choose their best word within the sentence. Here the emphasis is on the meaning of the words used and it is children's own choices that are used.

Summary of points for the class teacher

> ➢ It is important to plan for the purpose of the talk as well as for the topic of the talk.
> ➢ What you say to children is important. It is very easy to give the wrong impression about what is important.
> ➢ Make sure your introduction emphasises what you want children to concentrate on.
> ➢ Make sure what you say as you talk to individual writers emphasises what you want children to concentrate on.
> ➢ Make sure the feedback you give to writers about their writing emphasises what you want children to concentrate on.
> ➢ Don't feel you have to keep reminding them about spelling and punctuation. Our research shows that these aspects are very much in the forefront of their minds.
> ➢ Think about using props or other supports to help with the writing task.
> ➢ Remember that words are only good or bad in the context in which they are used.

Suggested further reading

Mercer, N. and Hodgkinson, S. (2008) *Exploring Talk in School: Inspired by the Work of Douglas Barnes*. London: SAGE.

Myhill, D., Jones, S. and Hopper, R. (2005) *Talking, Listening and Learning: Effective Talk in the Primary Classroom*. Maidenhead: Open University Press.

Interlude 4

My favourite lesson

Linda Bateman

Class teacher

The lesson I am focusing on is one I used successfully with a Year 1 class, but could easily be adapted to suit other ages. The task is particularly appropriate for a Year 1 class as it is a 'short burst' activity which allows for personalisation and differentiation.

There was a huge range of ability and a very high level of special needs in the class, including some children with statements of special needs for speech and language plus other general learning difficulties. There were also some children with English as an additional language who were in the early stages of English language acquisition.

The lesson was part of the wider topic of 'Yum, Yum!', which is based on food. We had been looking at the traditional tale of *Stone Soup*, where a man tricks visitors into giving him vegetables to make vegetable soup. Having read the story earlier in the week and discussed the moral, I told the children that we were to make some soup. I had a recipe to follow, with copies for all of them. I opened a folder to find that the recipes had disappeared and there was only blank paper (with a title and a border of vegetable pictures to help with idea generation) to be found!

At this point I asked for the children's help and tried their suggestions. One of my regular classroom props is a rather inefficient wizard puppet, who was called upon to help in his usual dramatic but inept way. After several attempts at spell-making we decided that he was unable to magic the recipe back. I had also made copies of the recipe for the children to use when making their soup, but these too had disappeared! The only thing for it was for each child to write their own so that we could use them in the cooking activity.

At this point, however, I then found a 'magic wand' (in fact a cocktail stirrer bought from the local supermarket, made of sparkly plastic with a star shape at the end). I had conveniently found these in packs of 10 (reduced as well!) and acquired 30 of them. I discovered that if I ran the star of my magic wand over the paper, I could just about make out what the words of the recipe said, and then quickly wrote the ingredient down before each item disappeared again.

We used this stage of the lesson as idea generation, accepting ideas from as many children as possible and adding them to the list of vegetables on the recipe sheet. From this, I gave each child their own magic wand and they then worked with a talk partner to 'read' their own recipe as an oral rehearsal.

A few of the children struggled with the concept of reading something which they could not see, but were helped by those who were most enthusiastic and were able to support them in the task. However, I did find that one or two, interestingly those with speech and language or Autistic Spectrum Disorders or difficulties, needed to be let in on the secret quietly and conspiratorially, so as not to spoil the magic for the others. Once they knew that it was a joke and that they had to 'pretend', they were happy to relax and enjoy it.

After this, I found it beneficial for the children to share with me and the rest of the class the first item in their recipe. I use this method on most writing tasks. It gives the children their first piece of writing, and once this is committed to paper the children are much more likely to be able to continue. It means that they do not have the issue of sitting in front of a blank piece of paper whilst all around them others get going. It also generates more ideas for those children who might not find the task easy, reinforcing the vocabulary needed. From this point of view it helps to know the children well: I would send each child off to begin after they had shared their ideas. Consequently, knowledge of the children helps to decide who needs to hear other children's ideas again, weighed against who needed to be off and writing.

I encourage children to think, say it, write it, at all times. Those that completed their recipe were then given the task of writing the method as a differentiated task. I would also read children's ideas to the rest of the class to provide them with further ideas and reinforce the success criteria for the lesson.

The plenary involved sharing ideas and discussing the 'tricky' bits of the task.

I used this idea several times with the same and subsequent classes and soon found that it was easy to think of variations. Some of the children were enchanted by their magic wands and requested them in independent writing tasks or during other sessions. I think for some it took the pressure off them: after all, the recipe had already been written, so they did not have the demanding task of starting from scratch: all they had to do was read it!

Appendix 1

The Research Report – Talk to Text: Using Talk To Support Writing

A project funded by the Esmée Fairbairn Foundation.

Dr Ros Fisher
Professor Debra Myhill
Dr Susan Jones
Dr Shirley Larkin

Graduate School of Education, University of Exeter

It is through language, especially spoken language, that teachers teach and children learn. (Alexander, 2004: 2)

Introduction

The Talk to Text Project was a project funded by the Esmée Fairbairn Foundation from December 2004 to the end of November 2006. Based on a social constructivist view of learning it sought to explore the relationship between classroom talk and writing in the early stages of children's schooling. Data collection was completed, as planned, by the end of June 2006 and dissemination began through conference papers in July 2006.

Aims

The principal aims of the project were to investigate how creating explicit opportunities for talk might enhance children's early attempts at writing, and to develop practical and successful ways of implementing this in the classroom.

Specific subsidiary aims were:

- To implement and evaluate the impact of using talk creatively (such as through drama) to generate ideas and motivation for writing

- To implement and evaluate the use of oral rehearsal of sentences as a preparation for writing

- To implement and evaluate the value of using talk to support reflection and metacognition (such as through shared writing, modelling and talking partners).

Project outline

The project was carried out in three phases. In the first year a pilot project was conducted which consisted of two phases. The first ran from December 2004 until April 2005 and was concerned with trialling data collection methods. The second phase ran from May 2005 until August 2005 and was concerned with the evaluation of the talk activities. A report on this two-stage pilot project was submitted in October 2005. Following the evaluation of the pilot project, two further schools joined the project.

Phase three was the main Talk to Text project and ran for one full school year from September 2005 until July 2006. A central element of the project was the close collaboration between teachers and university researchers. Four meetings were held during the year and the project website encouraged discussion between meetings.

Pilot study

The pilot proved very useful in the development of the main project in three main ways. First, the methods of data collection were trialled and initial problems with the recording of children's talk in a busy classroom were overcome. In particular, the use of external microphones attached to the video cameras proved the best way of recording spoken language and important paralinguistic information. Second, the talk activities were developed and trialled employing both existing teacher practice and new activities developed from theoretical understanding. Thirdly, the evaluation of the pilot enabled the university-based research team to manage the data collection in such a way that teachers felt able to improvise on basic ideas. This facilitated the continued development of successful talk activities over the period of data collection.

The main aims of the project involved the development and the evaluation of activities to encourage the use of talk to support writing. Thus there was a tension between a design that allowed development of useful activities and a research project that enabled comparative evaluation. Ultimately, the desire to produce practical outcomes that would be of benefit to the profession outweighed the need for a control group to test the effectiveness of the activities. Indeed, the enthusiasm of the schools for the project resulted in it being necessary to locate comparison classes outside of the project schools, resulting in real threats to the validity of control data.

Design of main project

Sample

The sample for the main project is set out in Table A.1.

Table A.1   Project classes

School code	No. of classes	Year group
A/W	2	1
B/W	1	2
D/W	1	1
E/P	1	2
F/P	1	1/2 mixed

In addition, Phase 3 involved two comparison classes from non-participating schools. These two classes were both Year 2. In total, 172 Year 1 and Year 2 children took part in the project.

In each class, six children were chosen by the class teacher to become a focus group for the collection of data. These groups were of mixed gender and represented an even split of low, middle and high attainment in literacy, as assessed by school-based measures. Six children from each of the two comparison classes were selected on the same basis, to provide a baseline comparison with the Talk to Text groups.

Data were collected on 36 children from the Talk to Text classes and 12 children from the comparison classes.

Data collection

Writing samples

At the beginning of the autumn term, 2005, teachers in all classes were asked to provide one piece of fiction and one piece of non-fiction writing for each child in their class. In order to facilitate comparisons across schools, the university research team asked that the fiction piece should be a re-telling of a well-known story and the non-fiction piece should be a letter welcoming a new child to the class. At the end of the project in summer 2006, two similar pieces of writing were collected from every child.

Child interviews

At the beginning and end of the project, university researchers conducted inter-views with all the focus group children. The children were interviewed in boy/girl pairs, with each pair representing low, middle or high attainment in literacy as assessed by their teacher. The purpose of the interviews was to explore:

- Children's attitudes towards writing
- Children's ability to evaluate good writing and good writing strategies
- Children's thoughts on the process of becoming a writer.

Children were initially shown pictures of children writing in class and asked to comment on the pictures. Following this, they were questioned according to the themes outlined above.

Observation and video data

University researchers visited the project schools each term during the year to observe the focus children. The observations included video-capture of the initial teacher whole-class input, then video capture of two of the focus children working on a Talk to Text activity. Field notes were recorded by the researcher at the time and later the researcher noted her reflections on the observation period. Photocopies of work produced by the focus children during that particular period were collected.

Teachers and head teachers were also encouraged to observe the focus children during the year and to collect video data of these children engaged in Talk to Text activities.

Teacher reflections

Teachers were asked to keep a reflective audio diary throughout the project.

Teacher interviews

All the project teachers were interviewed four months after the end of the project. The purpose of the interviews was (a) to explore teachers' individual views about teaching writing; and (b) to ascertain teachers' retrospective reflections on the outcomes of the project. Interviews were conducted in private. They lasted for about one hour and were audio-taped. The tapes were transcribed and the transcripts sent to teachers for verification.

Summary of data collection

In total, 736 scripts of children's writing were collected. Eighty-four scripts of children's fiction and non-fiction writing were scored at the start of the project and 54 scripts were scored at the end of the project (see data analysis below).

- 25 hours of video footage were collected and analysed.
- 48 children were interviewed at the beginning and end of the project.
- 13 audio and written reflections were collected from teachers.

Analysis of data

The rich data collected during the project enabled different kinds of mainly qualitative analysis.

Video data

The classroom observations captured on video were transferred to mpeg files and stored on the project laptop. The videos were analysed using ATLAS ti software. ATLAS ti is a visual qualitative data analysis package which can be used for data captured in different media. It also enables integration of different kinds of data. After consultation with CAQDAS (Computer Assisted Qualitative Data Analysis System) specialists, ATLAS was chosen as the best package for the needs of this project. The use of ATLAS enabled us to code directly onto video clips without the need to transform video data into text. As every time data is transformed, an interpretation takes place, the use of ATLAS allowed us to stay as close as possible to the live experience of the classroom. The video data is supplemented by the researchers' field notes and subsequent reflections and by the teachers' and head teachers' reflections. Video produces a great deal of information and coding is both time consuming and complex. The university research team met regularly to discuss the coding of the video data. Different frameworks were created, amended and re-created until a set of codes was agreed which captured most of the recurring behaviour relevant to the project's aims. This set of codes was then clustered into themes and networks of associations between themes were created.

Child interviews

The interviews were analysed initially according to the three themes:

- Children's attitudes towards writing
- Children's ability to evaluate good writing and good writing strategies
- Children's thoughts on the process of becoming a writer.

Thus the transcripts were coded according to whether the responses related to the child's attitudes to the activity of writing; their evaluation of the written product; or to their understanding of learning to write. Those responses relating to children's attitudes to writing were subdivided into positive and negative statements and into statements relating to ease or difficulty of writing. Responses relating to the evaluation of writing were split into those that focused on the writing and those that focused on the writer. These groups of statements were then further analysed to provide a more detailed picture of children's understandings.

In order to explore the relative importance of these understandings and the extent of any changes over the year of the project, frequency counts were made of the children's answers by category.

Writing samples

The writing samples of the focus group children were scored along the following dimensions: purpose and organisation, style, punctuation, spelling, handwriting. Stockport Levels (Stockport Metropolitan Borough Council, 2005) were amended to include some explications used by schools, and these amended levels were used to score the samples. Stockport Levels provide finer grading than QCA documentation and relate closely to National Curriculum levels. However, it was felt that using a combination of Stockport Levels and assessment criteria already in use in the schools would provide more specific grades. The initial scoring of a 20% sample of the scripts by two researchers achieved an inter-rater reliability of only 62%. As a result it was decided that the researchers should score all the scripts independently and then discuss discrepancies until 100% agreement was reached. The scores were entered into EXCEL. At the end of the project a random sample of scripts was sent to teachers and head teachers to score. The results of scoring and subsequent discussion by teachers raised serious doubts about the validity and reliability of such measures.

Teacher interviews

Six teachers from the project schools were interviewed four months after the end of the project in the schools. The interviews were audio-taped and transcribed. A qualitative analysis based on Activity Theory was carried out to identify key themes that could be said to influence teacher practice and how that practice may impact on pupils. Themes from the teacher interviews will be compared to those from pupil interviews and classroom video data.

Research findings

Video data
Using ATLAS ti allowed the research team to take a grounded approach to coding the video data. Each of the 24 hour-long videos was watched in its entirety to get a sense of the whole lesson. Then the video was sectioned into small clips and coded. New codes were added to the code list as they occurred in different videos until no new codes emerged.

The codes set out in Tables A.2–A.4 formed the basis of this analysis of talk during paired talk. Codes for teacher talk during whole class sessions were coded separately.

Table A.2   Codes focusing on child-to-child interaction

Code	Number of instances recorded
Child encourages/accepts other child's ideas/suggestions	22
Child asks child for help	26
Child comments on/evaluates other's/own writing/talk	27
Child ignores other child's idea/suggestion	10
Child observes other child writing	13
Child revises work – child prompted	2
Child shows/tells other child own writing	20
Children manage/talk about task	69
Children share ideas together	45
Children support oral rehearsal together	26
Children talk about writing/spelling/scribing	69
Getting ideas from/giving them to other children	6
Social talk	44

Table A.3   Codes focusing on individual children

Code	Number of instances recorded
Child expresses frustration/confusion	9
Child asks teacher for help	11
Child expresses task aspiration goal	1
Child gives ideas supported by teacher	30
Child oral rehearsal to capture thinking	23
Child reads out to perform	21
Child responds to teacher's question	6
Child revises work self-realised	7
Child reads out writing to generate ideas	18
Child re-forms sentence orally	2
Child revises work – teacher prompted	6
Child says sentence as they write	52
Child sounds out spelling	51
Child uses aid for spelling/writing	14
Child writes with magic pencil	7
Children being reflective	2
Children write/work silently	66

Table A.4   Codes focusing on the teacher

Code	Number of instances recorded
Teacher input relating to spelling/punctuation/ scribing	33
Teacher supports child-to-child interaction	23
Teacher summarises child's ideas	1
Teacher supports oral rehearsal	17
Teacher supports reflection	6
Teacher manages task	32
Teacher supports ideas and/or builds on content	29

Frequency counts of the behaviour corresponding to each code were made. It was decided that a count of 40 or more for a code would render that code one of the most common. The most common codes found in children's talk are shown in Table A.5.

Table A.5   The most common codes

Code	Number of recorded instances
Children manage or talk about the task	69
Children talk about writing, spelling or scribing	69
Child writes or works silently	66
Child says sentence as they write	52
Child sounds out spelling	51
Children share ideas together	45
Social talk	44

However, children from different attainment levels were found to appear differentially in the codes. Thus a further analysis by attainment level can be seen in Tables A.6–A.10.

Table A.6   The most common codes for the high attainment children

Code	Recorded instances for HA children as percentage of all instances
Children share ideas together	80%
Children support oral rehearsal together	69%
Encouraging or accepting other child's ideas	68%
Observing the other child writing	62%
Child says sentence as they write it	58%
Uses oral rehearsal to capture thinking	52%

Table A.7   The most common codes for the average attainment children

Code	Recorded instances for AA children as percentage of all instances
Child uses aid for spelling/writing	79%
Expresses frustration or confusion	78%
Reads out writing to generate ideas	44%
Social talk	43%

Table A.8   The most common codes for the low attainment children

Code	Recorded instances for LA children as percentage of all instances
Ignores other child's idea or suggestion	70%
Child asks child for help	42%
Sounds out spelling	45%

Table A.9   Codes focusing on the teacher (here the instances have been split to show which were observed in whole-class sessions and which during paired)

Code	Whole class	Paired work	Total
Teacher input relating to secretarial	12	33	45
Teacher supports talk	42	23	65
Teacher supports oral rehearsal/form	53	17	70
Teacher supports reflection	13	6	19
Teacher manages task	38	32	70
Teacher supports ideas and/or builds on content	74	30	104
All teacher codes	232	141	373

Table A.10   Teacher codes split according to writing attainment (paired work only)

Code	HA	AA	LA	Paired work total
Teacher input relating to secretarial	3	8	22	33
Teacher supports talk	12	5	6	23
Teacher supports oral rehearsal/form	1	8	8	17
Teacher supports reflection	1	1	4	6
Teacher manages task	8	12	12	32
Teacher supports ideas and/or builds on content	8	8	14	30
All teacher codes	33	42	66	141

Clustering codes

In moving to a second level of analysis, codes were clustered according to the kind of talk that was being engaged in rather than what the talk was about. The following clusters were developed:

Strategic: forward thinking
Definition: 'A strategy is originated by the writer and has the intention of having an effect on the user's writing.'

Evaluative: reflecting back
Definition: 'Talk is used to express a judgement on the context, the writing or the task.'

Constructive: current support
Definition: 'Talk used to support the writer in achieving the task.'

Details of these findings can be found in Chapter 5.

Child interviews

Details of these findings can be found in Chapter 7.

Writing samples

Overall, the research team felt that the measurement of progress through scoring of writing samples using National Curriculum descriptors was an unconvincing measure of the project children's achievement. Firstly, the process of scoring was felt to be very subjective and reliability checks confirmed this impression. Second, the writing tasks were chosen to be simple for young children to complete early in the year and easy to replicate on a second occasion. In retrospect, the project teachers did not feel that the tasks allowed pupils to display the imagination and creative use of language that the project had helped them to develop.

Further areas for investigation

Teacher practice

Early findings from the analysis of the video data reveal significant differences in the way the activities have been mediated by the teachers. Although each teacher used a variety of the project activities as well as their own favourites, the way in which each teacher introduced, taught and responded to the writing tasks varied considerably. Such variations seemed to impact on how children responded to the tasks. Close analysis of teacher practice together with analysis of children's behaviour and the writing samples suggests important recommendations for teachers that can be disseminated through the writing activity materials. Furthermore, this analysis will contribute to socio-cultural understandings of teacher practice.

Teacher involvement

The teachers and head teachers from the project schools have been fully involved in all aspects of the research project. They are also involved in the dissemination of the findings of the project. Two teachers, one from School A and one from School B, have written an article for *English 4–11*. They and other teachers have contributed to this book.

One of the project teachers was entered for the 'New Teacher of the Year' contest and won her regional final. When she was observed by the judges she chose to do one of the Talk to Text activities and the lesson was greatly praised by the judges.

Key outcomes for research, policy and practice

- The research will take forward our understanding of three key areas of theory:

  o Young children's metacognition in early writing
  o More detailed and specific understanding of the relationship between different talk activities and early writing
  o Understanding of the socio-cultural factors that impact on children's development as writers.

- The research has implications for practice:

  o The importance of teacher input in the management of talk activities prior to writing
  o The need for clarity about the purpose of the talk activities
  o The value of helping children to say sentences aloud prior to writing.

- Implications for policy are less well developed but indicate:

  o The importance of talk to support development in writing
  o The problematic nature of current assessment practices in writing.

Appendix 2

Child Interview Schedule

Purpose

The interviews are intended to explore children's views on:

- Quality of writing – presentational features, secretarial features, meaning based, personal reasons
- Attitudes to writing – positive/negative, analysing types found easy/difficult
- Strategies they employ – internal/external.

The interviews will follow a semi-structured format. The questions will focus on children's understanding of quality of writing; their attitudes to writing; their knowledge of strategies to help them write. Interviewers should ask the initial question and then prompt for answers related to the construct concerned (quality, attitudes, strategies). Interviewers should encourage children to speak at greater length by non-judgemental responses such as 'right', 'oh yes'; by waiting and allowing children to fill the silence; or by repeating the question using a similar question keeping the focus on the construct. Interviewers should avoid summarising what children have said and asking leading questions.

Analysis will involve simple coding of responses in relation to each of the three constructs.

Preamble

My name is … and I'm a researcher. I'm interested in finding out about children learning to write and I'd like to ask you some questions about writing. I will record your answers so that I can remember what you have said. I'm particularly interested in what you think about writing, how you get ideas and what helps you to do writing. You can stop being interviewed at any time. If you don't want to carry on or answer a question just tell me. Are you happy to help us with our research?

Begin recording

The first thing I'd like you to do is to look at this picture and tell me what you think these people are thinking. [(Researcher writes in the bubble or lets child do it). If the child writes, then:]

Q: Can you tell me what you have written?

Quality

Q: Do you think the person is a good writer? Why?
Q: Are you a good writer? How do you know that?

Now I will ask you both questions together. Anyone can answer and you can agree or disagree with each other if you like.

Q: Who are the good writers in the class? Why do you think that?

Attitude

Q: What do you enjoy about writing?
Q: Tell me what you don't enjoy about writing?
Q: What kinds of writing are hard to do? Why?
Q: What kinds of writing are easy to do? Why?

Strategy

Q: What helps you to do your writing?
Q: What do you do if you get stuck on a piece of writing?
Q: How do you think people learn to write?
Q: Is there anything else you would like to say about writing?

References

Alexander, R. (2004) *Towards Dialogic Teaching: Rethinking Classroom Talk*. Cambridge: Dialogos.

Baddeley, A.D. and Hitch, G.J.L. (1974) 'Working Memory', in G.A. Bower (ed.) *The Psychology of Learning and Motivation: Advances in Research and Theory, Vol. 8*. New York: Academic Press. pp. 47–89.

Barnett, A., Henderson, S.E., Scheib, B. and Schulz, J. (2009) 'Development and Standardisation of a New Handwriting Test: the Detailed Assessment of Speed of Handwriting', in V. Connelly, A. Barnett, J. Dockrell and A. Tolmie (eds) *Teaching and Learning Writing. Monograph Series 11: Psychological Aspects of Education – Current Trends No 6*. Leicester: British Psychological Society. pp. 137–58.

Bereiter, C. and Scardamalia, M. (1982) 'From Conversation to Composition: the Role of Instruction in a Developmental Process', in R. Glaser (ed.) *Advances in Instructional Psychology, Vol. 2*. Hillsdale, NJ: Lawrence Erlbaum Associates. pp.1–64.

Berninger, V.W., Fuller, F. and Whittaker, D. (1996) 'A Process Model of Writing Development across the Life Span', *Educational Psychology Review*, 8(3): 193–218.

Berninger, V., Vaughan, K., Abbott, R.D., Begay, K., Coleman, K.B., Curtin, G., Hawkins, J.M. and Graham, S. (2002) 'Teaching Spelling and Composition Alone and Together: Implications for the Simple View of Writing', *Journal of Educational Research*, 94(2): 291–304.

Bock, K. (1995) 'Sentence Production: From Mind to Mouth', in J.L. Miller and P.D. Eimas (eds) *Handbook of Perception and Cognition, Vol. 11: Speech, Language, and Communication*. Orlando: Academic Press. pp. 181–216.

Bock, K. and Levelt, W.J.M. (1994) 'Language Production: Grammatical Encoding', in M. Gernsbacher (ed.) *Handbook of Psycholinguistics*. New York: Academic Press. pp. 948–84.

Bourdin, B. and Fayol, M. (1994) 'Is Written Language Production Really More Difficult than Oral Language Production?', *International Journal of Psychology*, 29(5): 591–620.

Bourdin, B. and Fayol, M. (2002) 'Even in Adults, Written Production is Still More Costly than Oral Production', *International Journal of Psychology*, 37(4): 219–22.

Britton, J. (1970) *Language and Learning*. Harmondsworth: Penguin.

Capello, M. (2006) 'Under Construction: Voice and Identity Development in Writing Workshop', *Language Arts*, 83(6): 482–91.

Chaffee, A.J. (1977) 'The Ghostly Paradigm in Composition', *College English*, 39(4): 477–83.

Chan, L. (1998) 'Children's Understanding of the Formal and Functional Characteristics of Written Chinese', *Applied Psycholinguistics*, 19: 115–31.

Christie, F. (1987) 'Young Children's Writing: from Spoken to Written Genre', *Language and Education*, 1(1): 3–13.

Clark, L. (2000) 'Lessons from the Nursery: Children as Writers in Early Years Education', *Reading*, 34(2): 68–72.

Cleary, L.M. (1996) '"I Think I Know What my Teachers Want Now": Gender and Writing Motivation', *The English Journal*, 85(1): 50–7.

Connelly, V. and Hurst, G. (2001) 'The Influence of Handwriting Fluency on Writing Quality in Later Primary and Early Secondary Education', *Handwriting Review*, 2: 50–6.

Crystal, D. (1995) *The Cambridge Encyclopedia of the English Language*. Cambridge: Cambridge University Press.

DCSF (2009) *Primary National Strategy Literacy Framework*. http://nationalstrategies.standards.dcsf.gov.uk/primary/primaryframework/literacyframework (accessed 12 August, 2009).

Desforges, C., Bennett, N. and Cockburn, A.D. (1985) 'Understanding the Quality of Pupil Learning Experiences', in N.J. Entwhistle (ed.) *New Directions in Educational Psychology*. Lewes: Falmer Press.

Dyson, A.H. (2002) 'The Drinking God Factor: a Writing Development Remix for "All" Children', *Written Communication*, 19(4): 545–77.

Englert, C.S., Berry, R. and Dunsmore, K. (2001) 'Case Study of the Apprenticeship Process: Another Perspective on the Apprentice and the Scaffolding Metaphor', *Journal of Learning Disabilities*, 34(2): 152–71.

Fayol, M. (1991) 'Stories: a Psycholinguistic and Ontogenetic Approach to the Acquisition of Narrative Abilities', *Journal of Literary Semantics*, 20(2): 78–96.

Ferreiro, E. and Teberosky, A. (1982) *Literacy before Schooling*. Oxford: Heinemann.

Fisher, R. (2002) 'Shared Thinking: Metacognitive Modelling in the Literacy Hour', *Reading, Literacy and Language* (now called *Literacy*), 36 (2): 64–8.

Flower, L. (1979) 'Writer-Based Prose: a Cognitive Basis for Problems in Writing', *College English*, 41(1): 19–37.

Garton, A. and Pratt, C. (1989) *Learning to be Literate: the Development of Spoken and Written Language*. Oxford: Basil Blackwell.

Gathercole, S.E. (2004) 'Working Memory and Learning During the School Years', *Proceedings of the British Academy*, 125: 365–80.

Gathercole, S.E., Pickering, S.J., Ambridge, B. and Wearing, H. (2004) The Structure of Working Memory From 4 to 15 Years of Age. *Developmental Psychology*. 40(2) 177–90.

Gibson, E. and Levin, H. (1980) *The Psychology of Reading*. Cambridge, MA: MIT Press.

Gopnik, A. (2003) 'The Theory Theory as an Alternative to the Innateness Hypothesis', in L.M. Anthony and N. Hornstein (eds) *Chomsky and his Critics*. New York: Blackwell. pp. 238–54.

Hasan, R. (2002) 'Semiotic Mediation and Mental Development in Pluralistic Societies: Some Implications for Tomorrow's Schooling', in G. Wells and G. Claxton (eds) *Learning for Life in the 21st Century*. Oxford: Blackwell. pp. 112–26.

Hayes, J. and Flower, L. (1980) 'Identifying the Organization of Writing Processes', in L. Gregg and E. Steinberg (eds) *Cognitive Processes in Writing*. Hillsdale, NJ: Lawrence Erlbaum Associates. pp. 3–30.

Hayes, J.R. (2006) 'New Directions in Writing Theory', in C. Macarthur, S. Graham and J. Fitzgerald (eds) *Handbook of Writing Research*. New York: Guilford. pp. 28–40.

Israel, S.E., Collins Block, C., Bauserman, K.L., Kinnucan-Welsch, K. (eds) (2005) *Metacognition in Literacy Learning, Theory, Assessment, Instruction and Professional Development*. Mahwah, NJ: Lawrence Erlbaum.

Kellogg, R. (2008) 'Training Writing Skills: a Cognitive Development Perspective', *Journal of Writing Research*, 1(1): 1–26.

Kress, G. (1994) *Learning to Write*. London: Routledge.

Kress, G. (1997) *Before Writing: Rethinking the Paths to Literacy*. London: Routledge.

Larkin, S. (2010) *Metacognition in Young Children*. Abingdon: Routledge.

Lareau, A. (2003) *Unequal Childhoods*. Berkeley, CA: University of California Press.

Massey, A.J., Elliott, G.L. and Johnson, N.K. (2005) 'Variations in Aspects of Writing in 16+ English Examinations between 1980 and 2004: Vocabulary, Spelling, Punctuation, Sentence Structure, Non-Standard English', *Research Matters: Special Issue 1*. Cambridge: University of Cambridge Local Examinations Syndicate.

McCutcheon, D. (2006) 'Cognitive Factors in the Development of Children's Writing', in C. Macarthur, S. Graham and J. Fitzgerald (eds) *Handbook of Writing Research*. New York: Guilford Press. pp. 115–30.

Mortimore, P., Sammons, P., Stoll, L., Lewis, D. and Ecob, R.J. (1988) *School Matters: the Junior Years*. London: Open Books.

Murray, D.M. (1979) 'The Listening Eye: Reflections on the Writing Conference', *College English*, 41(1): 13–18.

Myhill, D., Jones, S. and Hopper, R. (eds) (2005) *Talking, Listening, Learning: Effective Talk in the Primary Classroom*. Buckingham: Open University Press.

Myhill, D.A. (2009a) 'Becoming a Designer: Trajectories of Linguistic Development', in R. Beard, D. Myhill, J. Riley and M. Nystrand (eds) *SAGE Handbook of Writing Development*. London: SAGE. pp. 402–14.

Myhill, D.A. (2009b) 'From Talking to Writing: Linguistic Development in Writing', in *Teaching and Learning Writing: Psychological Aspects of Education – Current Trends. British Journal of Educational Psychology*. Monograph Series II (6). Leicester: British Psychological Society.

Nixon, J.G. and Topping, K.J. (2001) 'Emergent Writing: the Impact of Structured Peer Assessment', *Educational Psychology*, 21(1): 42–55.

OECD (2002) *Educational Research and Development in England*. Paris: OECD.

Olson, D. (2006) 'Oral Discourse in a World of Literacy', *Research in the Teaching of English*, 41(2): 136–43.

Parr, J., Jesson, R. and McNaughton, S. (2009) 'Agency and Platform: the Relationships between Talk and Writing', in R. Beard, D. Myhill, J. Riley and M. Nystrand (eds) *SAGE Handbook of Writing Development*. London: SAGE. pp. 246–59.

Perera, K. (1984) *Children's Writing and Reading: Analysing Classroom Language*. Oxford: Blackwell.

Perera, K. (1986) 'Grammatical Differentiation between Speech and Writing in Children aged 8–12', in A. Wilkinson (ed.) *The Writing of Writing*. Milton Keynes. Open University Press: pp. 90–108.

Perera, K. (1987) *Understanding Language*. Sheffield: NAAE.

Prestage, S., Perks, P. and Soares, A. (2003) 'Developing Critical Intelligence: Tensions in the DfES Model for Best Practice Research Scholarship', *Educational Review*, 55(1): 55–63.

QCA/UKLA (2004) *More than Words*. London: QCA.

Schickendanz, J. and Casbergue, R. (2004) *Writing in Preschool: Learning to Orchestrate Meanings and Marks*. Newark, DE: IRA.

Stockport Metropolitan Borough Council (2005) Stockport LEA Writing level descriptors. Level 1. http://www.stockport.gov.uk./content/educationservices/teachers/curresources/stocklitstrat/litcentrearchive/ksI-2001?a=5441. (accessed 1 November, 2005).

Shanahan, T. (2006) 'Relations among Oral Language, Reading and Writing Development', in C. Macarthur, S. Graham and J. Fitzgerald (eds) *Handbook of Writing Research*. New York: Guilford Press. pp. 171–86.

Tolchinsky, L. (2006) 'The Emergence of Writing', in C. Macarthur, S. Graham and J. Fitzgerald (eds) *Handbook of Writing Research*. New York: Guilford Press. pp. 83–95.

Tolchinsky, L. and Cintas, C. (2001) 'The Development of Graphic Words in Written Spanish. What Can we Learn from Counterexamples?', in L. Tolchinsky (ed.) *Developmental Aspects of Learning to Write*. Dordrecht: Kluwer Academic Publishers. pp. 77–98.

Tucha, L., Tucha, O., Walitza, S., Kaunzinger, I. and Lange, K.W. (2007) 'Movement Execution during Neat Handwriting', *Handwriting Review*, 6: 44–8.

Index

Added to a page number 't' denotes a table

A

ability, learning to write 136–7
achievement groups
  on help with writing 140t
  on judging good writers 136
  on learning to write 138t
  talk patterns 88
action research, classroom talk 21–37
adverbial clauses 12t
adverbial connectives 12
appearance of writing, judging good writers
  135, 135t, 136t
Arabic 14
artefacts, using 46–7
articulatory rehearsal process 69
attitudes *see* children's attitudes
average achievers
  on help with writing 140t
  on judging good writers 136t
  on learning to write 138t
  talk patterns 88t

B

behaviour *see* pupil behaviour; writer's
  behaviour
Being Involved in Research – the View
  From a School 34–7
boys *see* gender

C

causal connectives 12, 13
child codes, for reflection 114–15t
child interview schedule 179–80
child talk, versus teacher talk 53–5
child-in-role 41, 156
child-to-child talk 91
children
  experiences of writing 1–2
  interviewing 31–3
children's attitudes
  researching 129–30
  to writing 130–1
children's stories 42
  using 13, 39–40, 41, 43–4, 75, 162
children's views
  judging good writers 134–6
  learning to write 136–8

Chomsky, Noam 13
circle time 156–7
classroom interaction 18, 24, 53
classroom observation 27–30
classroom talk
  action research 21–37
  impact on writing 89–92
  patterns 87–8
    in the focus lessons 92–4
    tracing ideas and sentences in 94–8
  see also constructive talk; evaluative
    talk; group talk; paired talk;
    strategic talk
classrooms
  exploring oral rehearsal in 71–5
  as writing communities 8–10
clauses 12t
co-constructed learning 86
co-constructed writing 52–3, 85, 117
cognitive demand, reducing 68–9
cognitive overload 5–6
cohesion 12t
collaborative writing 10, 48–52, 78,
  108, 117–18
colloquial forms, in writing 17
communities of writers 6–10
complex sentences 12t
composition
  oral rehearsal for 71–2, 74–5
  see also shared composition
Conscience Alley 41, 56–7, 75
constructive talk 86–7, 88, 88t, 92t
content of writing, difficulty with 132
context 13, 14, 15
control 119
creating text 69–71
Creating Text activity 2, 3

D

Department for Children, Schools
  and Families (DCSF) Standards
  website 64–5
descriptive sentences 164
developing writers 4, 5
development, learning to write 136–7
digital voice recording 78
discussion-based talk 159

E
effort, as a help with writing 139
egocentricity 13
emergent writers 6, 8
Emergent writing: the impact of structured peer interaction 10
emphasis, in writing 14
English as an Additional Language (EAL) 38, 41, 65, 75, 117
error correction 115
evaluating 120–2
Evaluating writing 144–5
evaluative talk 84–6, 88t, 92t
experiences
  drawing on 43–5
  need for metacognitive 111
expertise, in differing language structures 67
explicit guidance 18–19

F
feedback, in talk and writing 14
Field Place First School 34–7
finger-spacing 5, 134
first language speakers, middle-class 17
fluency, link between quality and 4
forum theatre 43, 58–9
forward thinking 84
freeze-frames 42, 60–1

G
gender
  on help with writing 140t
  on judging good writers 136t
  on learning to write 138t
  speed and fluency in writing 4
generative possibilities, of talk 19, 84, 87
genre, understanding of 7
"getting into role" 40–1
The Giant Postman 90–2
  paired talk in action 158
  talk patterns 92–3, 94
  tracing ideas and sentences 96, 97–8
girls *see* gender
graphemic units 5
graphic potential, of writing 15
group talk 66, 159
grouping for talk 159–60

H
hand-eye co-ordination 6
handwriting 4
Hayes and Flower model 2–4

high achievers
  on help with writing 140t
  on judging good writers 136t
  on learning to write 138t
  talk patterns 88
home literacy experiences 7–8
hot-seating 43
"how" questions 124

I
I Can't Ride my Bike 89–90, 98
  talk patterns 92, 93–4
  tracing ideas and sentences 95, 96–7
idea generation 22, 38–63
  co-construction of writing 52–3
  definition and example ixt
  in focus lessons 94–8
  lesson plans 56–63
  as a Planning activity 2
  talk activities 39–48, 89, 90
  talk for 153
  talk while writing 48–52
  teacher talk versus child talk 53–5
ideas
  spatial arrangements to convey 8
  testing and modelling 70
imagery 14
imaginative play, non-verbal 112
imaginative talk 66
initiation, response, feedback (IRF) 53–4, 156
instructions, giving 161–2
inter-textual talk 18–19
interactions
  idea generation 86
  scaffolding 18
  see also classroom interactions; peer interaction; social interactions
interpretation 6
interviews, with children 31–3
intonation 14, 71
Invisible Writing 100–1

K
knowledge, metacognitive 109

L
language
  and child-rearing styles 17
  for reflection 112–13
  structures, developing expertise in 67
language development
  social process 12–13
  in writing 11–12
LEAP Project 9

learning, as social endeavour 86
learning to write
    challenges 1
    children's views on 136–8
    early mark-making 6
lesson plans
    for idea generation 56–63
    for reflection 144–51
    for write aloud 100–7
A letter from the man in the
    moon 76–7
lexical items, in early writing 5
long-term memory 2
low achievers
    on help with writing 140t, 141
    on judging good writers 136t
    on learning to write 138t, 139
    talk patterns 88t

M
magic pencil 76–7, 89, 90, 102–3, 118
maps 155–6
mark-making, early 4–5, 6
meaning, in writing 6, 7
memory 2, 5–6, 68, 69
mental state words 112, 113
metacognition 22, 109–10, 114–25
metacognitive knowledge 109
metacognitive skill 109
middle-class first language
    speakers 17
mime 43
monitoring 109–10, 115–17, 119–20
monologic talk 13
monologic writing 13
multi-tasking activity, writing as 68
music, using 46, 62–3
My favourite lesson 166–7

N
names, writing 6–7
National Curriculum 8
National Literacy Strategy 19
National Writing Project 133
neatness
    as a barrier to fluency 4
    evaluating 85
"network of understandings" 7
non-lexical items, in early writing 5
non-Standard English, in writing 17
non-verbal communication 14
non-verbal imaginative play 112
non-verbal metacognition 117
noun phrases 12t, 13

O
"on a sea of talk" metaphor 18, 64
oral constructions 16–17
oral development, linked to writing
    development 18
oral expression, mismatch between
    writing and 68
oral rehearsal 22, 64–78
    in the classroom 71–5
    in policy documents 64–6
    research 66–71
    talk for 42, 153
    teaching activities 75–7
oral skills 82
orthography 4–5
others
    as a help with writing 139–40, 140t
    role, in learning to write 137, 138t
    writing for 13, 47–8

P
paired improvisation 43
paired talk 41, 42, 44, 47, 54–5, 157–9
paired writing 96, 104–5
paragraphs 12t
participation in communities of practice 9
    case study 10
partnership, working in 34–5
passive voice 11–12
passivity 141–2
pauses, in writing 3, 75
peer interaction 10
peer support, oral rehearsal to foster 73–4
perspectives, taking on other 111–12
pictures, using 45–6
pitch 14, 71
planning 117–18
    shift from the talk to writing context 153
    for talk for writing 156–9
Planning activity 2, 3
poetry writing 44
powerful words 163
practice, in learning to write 137
Primary National Strategy 19, 65
procedural facilitation and tools 8
    case study 10
prompt sheets 155
pupil behaviour, judging good writers
    135, 135t, 136t
puppets 41, 44, 154–5, 160

Q
Qualifications and Curriculum Authority (QCA) 7
quality, link between fluency and 4

questioning *see* self-questioning
questions
    facilitating metacognition 124–5
    investigating classroom practice 25t
    verbal responses to teachers' 112–13

R
reader-based prose 13
reader-writer relationship 13
readers, writing for 13
recording technology 78
reflection
    child and teacher codes 114–15t
    definition and example ixt
    developing language for 112–13
    lesson plans for 144–51
    talk for 153
    tasks for encouraging 110–12
    on writing 108
    see also metacognition
reflective talk 83
resources, as support for writing 139
Reviewing activity 3
revision, oral rehearsal as 66
role play 39–43, 44, 156

S
scaffolding 9, 18, 162
school literacy experiences 7–8
scribbling 6
scriptio continua 4, 6
secretarial aspects, of writing 52, 85, 108, 134
self
    as a help with writing 139, 140t
    in learning to write 138t
"Self as Writer" task 110–11
self-monitoring 119
self-questioning 123
sentences
    generating different versions 84
    language development 11, 12t
    oral rehearsal 65, 72–3
    paired construction 85
    structure 15
shared composition 19, 74–5
shared context 13, 15
"short burst writing" 153
skilled writers 4, 109, 122
social dialogue 18
social interactions 114
social practice, writing as 6–10
social process, language development 12–13
sociocognitive apprenticeships 8
    case study 9

spatial aspects, of writing 8
speech patterns, influence on writing 17
spelling 132
Standard English 17
A Step-by-Step Writing Guide 146–7
strategic talk 84, 88t, 92t
strategy, as a help with writing 139, 140t, 141
structured observation 27
systematic observation 29

T
talk
    differences between writing 14–15, 16t, 67
    features of 14
    importance in supporting early writing
        18–19
    influence on writing 16–17
    social nature 18
    while writing 48–52
    for writing
        grouping 159–60
        nature of tasks 153–4
        planning 156–9
        prompts to support 154–6
        purposes of 152–3
        see also idea generation; oral rehearsal;
           reflection
    see also classroom talk; paired talk
talk partners 114, 159
Talk to Text project viii-x, 5, 6, 18, 19, 168–78
    aims and purposes viii, 21, 168–9
    analysing examples of children's writing 30–1
    classroom observations 27–30
    classroom poster ix–x, xii
    data analysis 172–7
    data collection 170–2
    further areas of investigation 178
    idea generation 38–63
    interviewing the children 31–3
    managing talk 152–65
    oral rehearsal 64–78
    pilot study 169–70
    project outline 21–3, 169
    reflecting on writing 108–25
    researching children's views 128–42
    sample for main project 170
    teachers' involved in 20–1
    video data 23, 24–7, 117
    conclusions 33
Talking to a Toy 106–7
teacher codes, for reflection 114–15t
teacher modelling 9, 19, 77, 91, 95, 97, 113
teacher talk 53–5, 160–1
teacher-in-role 39–40, 156

teachers judgement, judging good
  writers 135t, 136t
teacher's questions, verbal responses to 112–13
teacher's role
  in fostering metacognition 124–5
  in learning to writing 137, 139–40
teaching
  activities for oral rehearsal 75–7
  feedback from children on 133
technologies
  communication of meaning 7
  forms of writing 1–2
telephone conversations 43
"telling others" 47–8
The Art of Reflection 126–7
"Thinking Cap" task 110, 148–9
thought tracking 42, 61
time-related connectives 12, 15
toys 158–9
transcription 6, 68–9
translating 2, 69–70
Two Ticks and a Wish 111, 150–1

U
United Kingdom Literacy Association
  (UKLA) 7
Using Write Aloud in the Classroom 80–1

V
verb phrases 12t
verbal, blending of visual and 7–8
verbal responses, to teachers' questions 112–13
video data 23, 24–7, 117
visual, blending of verbal and 7–8
visual nature, of writing 14–15
vocabulary 14, 67, 69

W
"what" questions 125
whole-class sessions
  paired talk 157
  reflective talk 83
whole-class talk 156–7
"why" questions 124–5
wondering aloud 158
words
  choosing 162–4
  developing writers understanding of 5

working memory (short-term) 5–6, 68, 69
"workshop" approach 10
write aloud 22, 66
  definition and example ixt
  lessons plans for 100–7
  using in the classroom 80–1
  see also oral rehearsal
writers
  children's views on judging good 134–6
  communities of 6–10
  differences between mature and
    developing 4
  see also developing writers; emergent writers;
    reader-writer relationship; skilled
    writers
writer's behaviour, judging good writers
  135t, 136t
writing
  analysing examples of 30–1
  children's attitudes to 130–1
  children's views on what helped with 138–41
  co-construction 52–3, 85, 117
  collaborative 10, 48–52, 78, 108, 117–18
  difficulty with mechanical aspects 131–2
  emphasis in 4
  Hayes and Flower model of 2–4
  home and school literacy practices 7–8
  language development in 11–12
  link between fluency and quality 4
  mismatch between oral expression
    and 68
  "on a sea of talk" metaphor 18, 64
  orthography 4–5
  pauses during 3, 75
  reducing cognitive demand 68–9
  scaffolding 162
  secretarial aspects 52, 85, 108, 134
  skills required 21
  as a social practice 6–10
  spatial layout 8
  and talk see talk
  transcription 6, 68–9
  young children's experiences of 1–2
  see also learning to write
writing communities 8–10
writing environment 2
writing process 2
writing-in-role 42–3